DOES MY GOLDFISH
KNOW WHO I AM?

Gemma Elwin Harris is a freelance editor and writer, as well as a mother, godmother and aunt to several extremely curious children. Her first book *Big Questions from Little People* (now out in paperback called *Why Can't I Tickle Myself?*) brought together great thinkers to answer kids' most searching, impossible or philosophical questions – in aid of leading children's charity the NSPCC.

The NSPCC is the only charity focused on ending child cruelty across the UK, driven by the simple belief that no child should suffer. Everything they do protects children and prevents abuse, helping children and families directly through local services, bringing immediate support through their national helplines, and providing training and support to people who work with children.

www.nspcc.co.uk

Does my GOLDFISH KNOW Who I AM?

COMPILED BY
Gemma Elwin Harris

WITH AN INTRODUCTION BY
Alexander Armstrong

FABER & FABER

First published in 2013
by Faber and Faber Limited
Bloomsbury House
74–77 Great Russell Street
London WC1B 3DA

This paperback edition first published in 2014

Typeset by Faber and Faber Limited
Printed in the UK by CPI Group (UK) Ltd, Croydon, CR0 4YY

A CIP record for this book
is available from the British Library

ISBN 978–0–571–30194–2

10 9 8 7 6 5 4 3 2 1

For Flo Po and Eliza

CONTENTS

THANK YOU FROM THE EDITOR

From asteroids to zebras, farts to football, via the human condition . . . this book tackles some very tricky questions from children on (just about!) every subject in the solar system. So a very warm thank you to all the brilliant and much-loved experts who made time to answer one for this project that benefits leading children's charity, the NSPCC (National Society for the Prevention of Cruelty to Children).

Many have now generously contributed to both this book and its predecessor *Big Questions from Little People*, for which we're extremely grateful. Particular thanks to Jim Al-Khalili, Sir David Attenborough, Heston Blumenthal, Derren Brown, Noam Chomsky, Marcus Chown, Heather Couper, David Crystal, Marcus du Sautoy, Alys Fowler, Joy Gaylinn Reidenberg, A. C. Grayling, John Gribbin, Bear Grylls, Celia Haddon, Claudia Hammond, Miranda Hart, Adam Hart-Davis, Bettany Hughes,

Kate Humble, Karen James, Annabel Karmel, Steve Leonard, Gary Marcus, George McGavin, Neil Oliver, Justin Pollard, Christopher Riley, Mary Roach, Alice Roberts, Simon Singh, Dan Snow, Gabrielle Walker and Yan Wong.

As for the curious minds behind the questions . . . children from all over the UK sent them in by their thousands. A special hello to participating schools: Corstorphine Primary, Portobello High, James Gillespie's, and Mary Erskine and Stewart's Melville Junior School in Edinburgh; Cleobury Mortimer Primary School, Shropshire; Landscove Primary, Devon; Woodland Grange Primary, Leicester; Furzedown Primary, Tooting; Raysfield Infants' School, Chipping Sodbury; Shottermill Junior, Haslemere; Boxgrove Primary School, Guildford; Grange Primary, Newham; Malvern St James Prep; The Mulberry Primary School, Tottenham; Notting Hill Prep; Lowther Primary, Richmond; and George Tomlinson Primary, Leytonstone.

Thanks, too, to the agents who made it all happen. Notably Jo Wander, Sophie Kingston-Smith, Celia Hayley, Verity O'Brien, Jonny Geller, Stephen Vishnick, Caroline Dawnay, Jo Sarsby, Anthony Arnove and Juliette Meinrath. For generous words, Jamie Byng; endless favours, Bex and Adam Balon;

and help with knotty science problems, Sophie Elwin Harris and Lucinda Middleton.

I'm indebted to Gordon Wise for sound advice and creativity over both books, and my editor Hannah Griffiths, who's brimful of energy and great ideas as ever – along with the rest of the talented folk at Faber: Donna Payne, Anna Pallai, John Grindrod, Matt Haslum and Kate Ward. Also Eleanor Rees for fine-tuning, Andy Smith for our eye-popping covers, and Stephanie Pollard of Visual Artefact, who fathomed the quiz answers in tandem with Justin Pollard.

Above all, a resounding cheer for staff at the NSPCC and the inspiring work you do protecting vulnerable youngsters. Charly Meehan, I'll miss working with you! Thank you also to Helen Carpenter, Lucie Sitch and team; Sarah Dade, Dan Brett-Schneider and the Fundraising Communications team; Julian Beynon; and Carol Thay. Here's to more than £100,000 raised by the Big Questions project at time of press in support of that work and, we all hope, much more to come.

Gemma Elwin Harris, 2013

INTRODUCTION

I am frequently guilty of doling out facetious – or worse, lazy – answers to my children's questions. To be fair this is sometimes because they are questions that don't really have answers; all parents get used to the cycle of 'but why?' questions with which our young explore the limits of our knowledge and our patience at one and the same time. But sometimes the questions are incisive, thoughtful and generally deserving of a better answer than that which my patchy understanding of aeronautics/professional wrestling/alchemy can supply. That is why this book is invaluable, and not just as an arsenal against future questions from the back of the car. This tome provides solid and reliable plugs to fit snugly into the myriad gaps in our knowledge that perhaps we'd prefer not to own up to – even to our children.

Alexander Armstrong, 2013

DOES MY GOLDFISH
KNOW WHO I AM?

DOES THE UNIVERSE HAVE AN EDGE?

ASKED BY Josh, age 10

Professor Brian Cox, *particle physicist, says:*

That's a great question. The answer is that we don't even know how big the Universe is! We can only see a small part of our Universe – the part that light has had the time to travel across to reach us during the 13.8 billion years since the Big Bang. Anything further away can't be seen, simply because the light from these distant places hasn't reached us yet.

The part we can see is pretty large, however. It contains around 350 billion large galaxies, each containing anything up to a trillion suns. This part, which is known as the observable Universe, is just over 90 billion light years across. But we are sure that the Universe extends far beyond this. It may even be infinitely big, which is impossible to imagine!

WILL MONKEYS EVER TURN INTO MEN?

ASKED BY Evie, age 6

Sir David Attenborough, *naturalist, says:*

Monkeys are very good at living in trees. They have hands and feet with which they can clamber about and pick the leaves and fruit they eat. No other animals, including human beings, can do it better than they do. So there is no need for them to change.

But things could alter. The forests could slowly get smaller so that there is less room for monkeys. Or a particularly good food might appear on the grassy plains beyond the forest edge. Then some monkeys might find it worthwhile to leave the forest and live out on the plain. If they did, then over millions of years they would slowly change. They would no longer need to grip branches. Instead they'd run about on the ground.

So their feet would become flatter, their legs longer, and they would stand upright. That is what may have happened to some apes a very long time ago. As millions of years passed, their bodies

3

altered. They became more and more like us. They were our ancestors.

But as long as monkeys have plenty of food in the forests and the forests themselves are big enough to provide them with homes, they will remain monkeys.

WHY DO I GET DIZZY WHEN I SPIN AROUND?

ASKED BY Jumaina, age 7

Dr Ellie Cannon, *GP and telly doctor, says:*

You may not know it but your balance and steadiness is actually controlled by your ears. They do the listening and they do the balance. Pretty clever really.

Right inside your ear, just next to your brain, there are three tiny tubes in an arch shape, full of liquid.

The tubes are lined with even tinier hairs that waft around in the liquid, a bit like plants under the sea. Those hairs are actually sending signals to your brain to say 'We're moving a lot today,' or 'We're not moving very much.'

If you're not moving, then the liquid is calm like a quiet pond and the hairs tell your brain that you're steady on your feet or sitting still. When you start spinning, that fluid gets really churned up like a stormy sea, and the hairs move wildly and tell your brain that you're spinning around. Trouble is, even when you stop spinning, that liquid carries on sloshing around for a while.

It takes a while to stop the sloshing – so the hairs keep sending those messages to say you're moving. Your body has stopped, but your brain still thinks you're moving. The difference between what your brain thinks and what your body is doing makes you feel dizzy.

I used to love doing this when I was a kid, though I always ended up crashing into my mum's coffee table.

HOW DO I KNOW MY LIFE ISN'T JUST A DREAM?

ASKED BY Esther, age 5

Derren Brown, *illusionist, says:*

Often we have dreams and they feel so real that we might wonder whether we're dreaming right now too. It feels like you're wide awake now, but doesn't it feel like you're wide awake in dreams too? How on Earth can you tell the difference? Maybe you'll wake up in a moment and realise you weren't reading this book – because it never existed!

Well, at least you know you're probably real. Because even if you were having a dream right now, there would have to be a you somewhere who was having that dream about yourself. But before your head starts spinning too fast, here's the important thought. We only ever really know about the stuff we see and hear and feel, and that's only a tiny part of what's around us. (For example, you can't see what's happening in the next room, or in someone else's head.) We can only guess at what's real from the little bit we know about – and often we get it very wrong.

So next time you have an argument or think someone's being stupid, remember: the other person is just as certain they're right, and really you only have half the story! So even though you're probably not dreaming, it's worth remembering that you're only aware of a small part of what's real, too.

WHAT WAS THE FIRST MUSICAL INSTRUMENT?

ASKED BY Caitlin, age 9

Tony Robinson, *actor, writer and broadcaster, says:*

When you're asked a question, it's rude not to answer, isn't it? Well, maybe. But sometimes if it's a difficult question like this one, the sensible thing is just to ask another question back, like 'What's a musical instrument?' or 'How do archaeologists know when they've found one?'

When we clap our hands, are they musical instruments? If so, the oldest instrument ever found has got to be the hands from an ancient skeleton. And how about stones? If you whack one, it'll make a noise. If you whack a smaller one, it'll make a different noise. Put three together and you've got a xylophone. But you're not going to put them in a case and take them to your music lessons, are you? You'll just chuck them away when you've finished playing them. They're a kind of temporary musical instrument.

Maybe what we mean by a musical instrument is something specially made and kept just for making music, and there are certainly 45,000-year-old bits of hollow bone with holes in that look suspiciously like early flutes. But maybe they're not. Perhaps the holes were drilled for a completely different reason. Maybe they were tools or jewellery or children's toys.

The most we can say for certain is that by around 35,000 years ago people were bashing drums, knocking out tunes on their xylophones, and blowing flutes and pipes made from vultures' wing bones and mammoths' tusks. Life must have been extremely noisy back then.

HOW CAN I BECOME A FOOTBALLER?

ASKED BY Azaan, age 7

Lee Dixon, *former Arsenal and England international, now TV football analyst, says:*

When I was a young boy of about seven or eight, growing up in Manchester, all I ever did was play football. I played at school. I played in the park. I played in the street. It was safe to do so back then as the streets were quieter and Mum could keep an eye on me. We even played in the house when it was raining with a balloon instead of a ball.

I wanted to be a footballer from my earliest memory. My dad was a professional for my favourite team, Manchester City, back in the 1950s. Also when I was young the best film that has ever been made was released: *Willy Wonka and the Chocolate Factory*. I watched it every time it was on and was fascinated by the Golden Tickets in the chocolate bars. So much so that I dreamed there was another golden ticket. This one didn't get you access to Willy's factory, however. This one got you a professional contract to play for Man City! How good is that?

It wasn't true, of course. There was no Golden Ticket. But nonetheless I used that dream to inspire me and I worked very, very hard at my football and eventually got a lucky break and signed a professional contract with Burnley FC in July 1983.

Throughout my career playing football, whenever I had a setback I thought about my dream. I knew if I worked hard and concentrated, there would be another chance. Another Golden Ticket. It has served me well.

CAN ANYTHING SURVIVE IN A BLACK HOLE?

ASKED BY Anthony, age 8, and Lauren, age 10

Marcus Chown, *author of books about space and the Universe, says:*

If you were in a spacecraft, you might be able to survive inside a black hole. But only if it was a big black hole and only for a short time.

A black hole is a region of space where gravity is so strong nothing can escape, not even light, so it appears black. If you approach a small black hole, only a few times as massive as the Sun, its gravity will stretch you out like a long piece of spaghetti and rip you apart. Surprisingly, though, big black holes are gentler. If you approach a 'supermassive' black hole – and many galaxies like our Milky Way contain holes billions of times bigger than the Sun – you will be able to pass into the hole with no ill effect.

Inside, it is a very dangerous place because lots of rocks and stuff from around the hole are falling in with you. Everything is heading towards the 'singularity' – the centre of the black hole lurking like a monstrous spider. Even if your spacecraft has the most powerful rocket engines imaginable, it cannot avoid being dragged there too.

A singularity crushes everything out of existence. But there is a small ray of hope. As black holes grow old, their singularities become less terrible. Some scientists think it might be possible to pass through them without being killed. The singularity may become a 'gateway' to another region of space and you could come out in an entirely new universe!

WHAT ARE HUMANS FOR?

<small>ASKED BY</small> Laszlo, age 5

A. C. Grayling, *philosopher, says:*

Humans are not 'for' anything, in the sense in which cows are farmed for their milk and meat and sheep are bred for their wool. But human beings can certainly have purposes and aims. Living so that we fulfil our aims is what gives our lives their meaning. We should never use other people as 'for' something, but should treat each person as worthwhile and respect them for the good that they try to do for themselves and others.

WHY DO WE HAVE RECESSIONS WHEN WE CAN PRINT MORE MONEY?

ASKED BY Cameron, age 11, and Mayur, age 9

John Lanchester, *author, says:*

Sometimes a government does print more money to try to end a recession, and sometimes it works!

In fact, one of the ideas being discussed in America right now is that the government should mint a special coin, worth one trillion dollars, in order to pay off all its debts! (A trillion is a very big number: it's a thousand thousand millions, or 1,000,000,000,000.)

But the thing that causes recessions isn't how much money there is in a country, it's whether people are spending it. When people are worried about the future, they often stop spending money and save it instead. If everybody does that at the same time, businesses make less money from selling their goods, and have less to pay their workers. Then the workers have less money to spend, and you have a recession. So just printing more money doesn't necessarily help people to feel more secure about the future.

The thing that ends recessions is when people feel more confident and start to spend a bit more, and everything picks up again.

WHY CAN'T WE DRINK WEE?

ASKED BY Isobel, age 4, and Leah, age 12

Bear Grylls, *explorer and survival expert, says:*

Now if you asked most normal people if they would drink their own wee they would look at you like you were mad. But here's the thing, if you are well hydrated but you have recently run out of water in a desert, drinking your own wee can definitely help save your life. Just don't expect it to taste nice!

There are a few key points to remember: if your wee is dark brown then it means you are already badly dehydrated and drinking it won't help you. At this stage it is total waste product expelled from your body. But if your wee is nice and clear then drinking it will help hydrate you.

There are many stories of people lost in deserts or stranded in a life raft at sea who have resorted to drinking their own wee and it has helped save them. So remember: those who survive are often those who can face the unimaginable and eat and drink the truly disgusting. If the worst comes to the worst, you just have to summon up the courage and do it!

HOW DOES THE LADY IN THE SATNAV KNOW WHERE SHE'S GOING?

ASKED BY Anaya, age 6

Ken Denmead, *'Geek Dad' author and blogger, says:*

The 'lady in the satnav' is really just the voice of a special little computer. The computer could talk to you in a man's voice, too; or a kid's voice, or even Darth Vader's voice!

The satnav itself is a pretty cool machine. It sends a radio signal up to a satellite orbiting the Earth, which keeps bouncing back to tell it exactly where it is at every moment. It also has maps stored in it that list every single address of every building and keep track of every road, roundabout, train station, airport and more.

If you ask it how to get to a place, it looks at the address, looks at exactly where you are at that moment, traces every possible route you could take to get from where you are to where you want to go, and then calculates which one will be the fastest. It may even get traffic reports and include them in its calculation, which is pretty smart!

Just remember that when you use a satnav, you should also pay attention to signs and signals. Sometimes there can be roadworks or special events that block or change streets in ways the satnav hasn't learned about yet. But it's a very useful little machine for helping you get where you want to go.

CAN YOU CREATE A SONG OUT OF ANYTHING?

ASKED BY Ethan, age 10

Sir Paul McCartney, *musician, singer and songwriter, says:*

Yes, just about anything! What about 'The Dancing Rubbish Bin'?

DO SPIDERS SPEAK?

ASKED BY Eleanor, age 7

Dr George McGavin, *entomologist (insect expert), says:*

Spiders do not speak like you and I, but they do communicate with each other.

Some spiders make visual signals that other spiders can understand. Jumping spiders, for example, have two particularly large eyes at the front of their head. They use these eyes to stalk insect prey but also when male and female spiders meet. If a male wants to be accepted as a mate by a female of the same species he must give the correct signals, such as dancing in front of the female in a particular way. Each species has a special dance, which the female watches very carefully. If the male gets it wrong or fails to impress her she will lose interest and walk away.

In many spiders, however, communication is based on what they can feel. The bodies of spiders are covered with many touch-sensitive hairs, which respond to all kinds of vibrations carried through their silk or through the air, so they can sense the presence of other animals, including other spiders of course.

WHO THOUGHT UP THE IDEA OF KINGS AND QUEENS?

ASKED BY Florence, age 10

Jeremy Paxman, *journalist, author and broadcaster, says:*

An anthropologist once tried to discover who'd thought up the idea of kings and queens. He gave up when he discovered that right back at the time of the earliest events ever recorded, there were already kings and queens.

Obviously the system began with someone tough enough or greedy enough to seize power and who then decided he wanted to pass it on to his children. Of course, it's not an arrangement we'd dream up now. But it works. The queen has no power, and only one job: to make people feel happier. It's not a bad thing to have someone do. And why give some politician the satisfaction of claiming to represent the whole nation?

WHAT IS DNA?

ASKED BY Max, age 9

Sam Kean, *author of science books, says:*

Let's say you want to remember your favourite recipe. (Trifle? Biscuits? Banoffee pie?) What do you do? If you're smart, you write the recipe down and put it somewhere safe. Your body does the same thing: whenever your cells need to remember how to do something important, they write the instructions down in what's called deoxyribonucleic acid, or DNA.

DNA works a lot like a language, like English. But while English has twenty-six letters in its alphabet, DNA has just four letters, called A, C, G and T. Those letters stand for the names of four chemicals, and by arranging the four letters in different orders, your body can spell out 'words' and 'sentences' that help your cells remember how to build and run your body. You get half your DNA from your mum, half from your dad, which explains why you look like them.

Something else that scientists talk about, along with DNA, is genes. A gene is a long stretch of

DNA – like a paragraph – and each of the 23,000 or so genes in your body is like a recipe for building one thing, usually a protein. Those proteins help form your muscles and bones and organs. They also influence nearly everything about you, from the colour of your hair to whether or not trifle really is your favourite food. Perhaps *you* prefer broccoli.

WHY DO MY FINGERS GO WRINKLY IN THE BATH?

ASKED BY Angus, age 11, and Joe, age 9

Dr Tom Smulders, *evolutionary biologist, says:*

When you soak in a warm bath for a little while – more than about fifteen minutes – the skin on your fingers and toes starts wrinkling. The same would happen if you did the dishes for a while. (Try it: your parents will love you for it!) So why does this happen?

Many people assume that the skin on the fingers and toes swells up because it absorbs water. But recent research has shown that instead of the fingertips getting bigger, as they would if they absorbed water, they in fact get smaller. Your fingers are wrinkly for the same reason that raisins and prunes are wrinkly: the inside of the finger has shrunk, so the skin is now too big to contain it, and wrinkles up.

What, then, makes the fingers shrink? It seems to be the blood vessels in your fingers and toes getting narrower. Narrower blood vessels mean less blood, and therefore a thinner (and wrinklier) finger.

The next question then is: what good is this wrinkling? Does the wrinkling get us anything? The answer to that question is not completely clear yet. It could be that the narrowing of the blood vessels is somehow helpful in itself, and that the wrinkles are just a side effect. However, in a recent experiment, we have shown that people have a better grip on wet objects when their fingers are wrinkled than when they are not.

This suggests that the wrinkling of the fingers may give us a better grip in wet conditions. Our primate ancestors may have benefited from wrinkly fingers when climbing through wet forests and trying to grab onto wet branches, with hands and feet.

If that is so, other primates (apes and monkeys) should also get wrinkly fingers and toes when wet, but we don't know yet whether that is true or not. Another science mystery waiting to be solved . . .

IF YOU SHOUTED IN SPACE WOULD YOU HEAR ANYTHING?

ASKED BY Matt, age 10

Ben Miller, *comedian, actor and science writer, says:*

I beg your pardon?

Only joking. To answer this question properly we are going to explore some fascinating science.

Firstly, what is sound? The answer is not as simple as you might think. Sound, it turns out, is a sort of pressure wave. It is created when an object vibrates in either a solid, a liquid or a gas.

Say you're listening to a song on speakers. The paper cone in the loudspeaker might vibrate and make pressure waves in the air, which are picked up by your ears and sent to your brain as tiny electrical signals that it understands as the words 'Hey sexy lady' from 'Gangnam Style'.

Sound travels pretty well in a gas like the air. But it travels even better in a liquid like water, and even better than that in a solid like, say, a tabletop. In fact, if you have a music device like an iPod, you can test this for yourself. Put the iPod on a tabletop and put your ear to the wood. Pretty loud, huh?

Of course in space there isn't any air, let alone water or wood, for the sound waves to travel through. So if you shouted in space, and you weren't wearing a helmet, your vocal cords wouldn't have anything to make pressure waves in, and so wouldn't make a normal shouting sound. Anything you did hear would be from sound waves travelling through your own head, and that would mean a much quieter, more muffled sound. It's dangerous to take your helmet off in space, so I don't think anyone has ever tried it.

If you shouted inside your space helmet, you would hear a proper shout, because the sound waves would have some air to travel through before they reached your ear.

But here's the weird bit. Any other astronauts that happened to be with you wouldn't hear a thing, because there wouldn't be any air to carry your shout to them.

Which is why they say that in space, no one can hear you scream. Spooky eh?

WHY IS IT FUNNY WHEN SOMEONE FARTS?

ASKED BY Alice, age 9

Miranda Hart, *comedian, writer and actress, says:*

What a silly question but a brilliant one. And I feel I am just the person to answer for, I hope like you, I find farting hilarious. It shouldn't be, should it? It's something we all do, to varying degrees. It's part of our biology. Yet most people on hearing one will burst out laughing. (Those who don't are weird in my opinion.)

I think the answer is because it is both naughty and embarrassing. Humans over the years have decided that farting should not be a public activity. So if we hear someone blow off we laugh because we know it to be 'wrong'. It is doubly funny when it is embarrassing.

When would it be really bad to fart? As you walked up the aisle at your wedding? If you met the Queen? A curtsey and . . . The more important the moment the funnier. Oh and finally, farts have varying trumpet-like noises and indeed lengths, all of which seem to have perfect comedy timing. And they come from a bottom. You might now ask: what's NOT funny when someone farts?

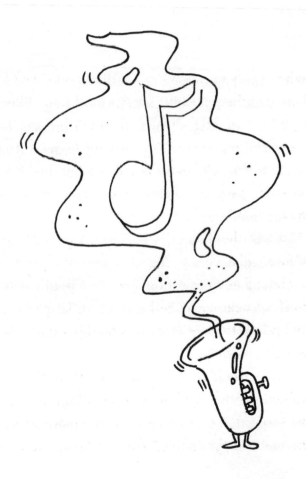

WHAT RUNS FASTER, A VELOCIRAPTOR OR A CHEETAH?

ASKED BY Lucas, age 5

Paul Geraghty, *author, illustrator and dinosaur expert, says:*

If a Velociraptor were here today, the race wouldn't even be close; the cheetah would win so easily.

With four spring-loaded legs and a long, bendy body, the cheetah can run in great leaping bounds at about 115 kilometres per hour.

The much smaller Velociraptor, at less than a metre high, could only run *dit-dit-dit-dit!* on two legs, like a miniature ostrich, probably at about half the speed of a cheetah.

Before you get disappointed, this is still much faster than a person has ever sprinted!

There are other dinosaurs we think would have been quicker than Velociraptor. The ostrich-like ornithomimids, for example (Gallimumus, Struthiomimus, Dromiceiomimus) and the ornithopod Hypsilophodon. But these, too, would easily be beaten by the cheetah.

IS NEW TECHNOLOGY ALWAYS GOOD?

ASKED BY Honor, age 11

Noam Chomsky, *linguist and philosopher, says:*

Technology is usually fairly neutral. It's like a hammer, which can be used to build a house or to destroy someone's home. The hammer doesn't care. It is almost always up to us to determine whether the technology is good or bad.

WHY ARE KIWIS HAIRY?

ASKED BY Evie, age 5

Alys Fowler, *gardening writer and broadcaster, says:*

To understand why kiwis are hairy, you are going to have to imagine that you are a very, very small insect. Perhaps an aphid, which is about the size of a pinhead. The world is very different when you are that small.

Now imagine you're feeling thirsty. Ideally you'd like a smoothie; something refreshing and nutritious to sup upon. You spy a huge vine with lots of lovely baby kiwi fruit growing all over it. 'That would make a perfect smoothie!' you think. So you land on a kiwi, only to find the surface is covered in a forest of hairs so thick that you cannot pierce the fruit, no matter how you try. And it's so bristly that it hurts your legs, so you leave.

The kiwi's hairy outside protects the insides. Those little black bits you see inside a kiwi are the seeds and this is what the plant is trying to protect. The seeds need to sit surrounded by the nice juicy fruit until they are ripe. If an insect robs the juicy bits, the seeds may not develop properly.

You can actually eat the coat of a kiwi. It's very nutritious but most people don't like the furry feel in their mouth. Not all kiwis are hairy. Some species are very small, the size of a strawberry, and have very little hair.

WHEN LIGHTNING STRIKES THE SEA, WHY DON'T FISH DIE?

ASKED BY Gabrielle, age 12

Professor Jim Al-Khalili, *scientist and broadcaster, says:*

This is because water conducts electricity so well, especially salty sea water. When lightning strikes the surface of the water, a tremendous amount of electric charge lands in the sea. But the important thing to remember is that the sea is very big and so the electricity can quickly spread out and get 'diluted'.

Imagine putting a drop of ink into a glass of water – the water will change colour. Now what if you put the same tiny amount of ink into a swimming pool? It will quickly spread out and you won't notice any difference in the colour of the water. The same idea applies to the electric charge from the lightning. Any one small part of the sea only has a tiny bit of electric charge, so a fish won't feel the full force of the lightning.

Of course, fish *would* die if they happened to be swimming very close to the spot where the lightning struck, before the electricity had a chance to disperse.

WHY DO WE HAVE RIGHTS AND LEFTS?

ASKED BY Peggy, age 6

Justin Pollard, *QI writer, says:*

Animals display several types of symmetry in their shapes. Some, like sea anemones, have what is called radial symmetry, with similar parts arranged around the centre of their body, where the mouth usually is. Some, like sponges, aren't symmetrical at all. But most animals have what is called bilateral symmetry, which means that they are made of two halves which are mirror images of each other. So we have two eyes, two nostrils, two arms and so on.

Our names for each side are known, rather splendidly, as 'egocentric co-ordinates'. This is because directions like 'left' and right' depend on us, not things outside of us – unlike, say, north or south. North is always north regardless of which way we're looking but if we look north then the east is on our right. If we look south then the east is on our left.

The Australian Guugu Yimithirr people don't use egocentric co-ordinates at all so they don't have 'left' and 'right'. They use compass points instead. Rather than say, 'The ticket is in my left pocket,' they might say, 'The ticket is in my east pocket.'

HOW DO INVISIBLE INKS WORK?

ASKED BY Ridhima, age 7

Dr Simon Singh, *science writer, says:*

A Roman scientist and general called Pliny the Elder was the first person to write about invisible inks. His recipe involved a pale juice extracted from a plant. This juice can be used to write on paper, and then it becomes transparent after drying. In order to reveal the message, the reader simply has to heat the paper, being careful not to burn it. The transparent ink then turns black. The ink darkens because it contains carbon, an element that turns black when it is heated.

You can experiment with invisible inks using any liquid that contains carbon, such as lemon juice, milk or even urine (also known as wee). Probably better to try lemon juice or milk. Use any fine point, such as a toothpick, as your pen and dip it into the liquid. After it has dried, you can reveal the message using a hot iron. Of course, make sure you have an adult to help you and be careful not to burn the paper or yourself.

You can write on blank paper when you experiment with invisible inks, but anybody who finds the paper will immediately be suspicious, because nobody sends blank paper to a friend. So, for serious secrecy, write a normal message first using normal ink, with plenty of space between the lines. Then write the invisible message in between the lines. Good luck with your experiments.

WHY DO LEAVES ONLY FALL IN AUTUMN?

ASKED BY Aksha and Lulu, age 9, Bruno, age 8, and Calum, age 5

Carol Klein, *gardening writer and broadcaster, says:*

In countries where the climate is cold in winter and warm in summer, lots of trees are deciduous, which means they lose their leaves in autumn.

Leaves grow in the spring and summer, but to keep them going through really cold weather would use enormous amounts of energy. So the tree adopts a plan of shedding all its leaves. The lovely autumn colours we see are part of the dying process. The sap inside the tree goes down into the roots. At the point where the leaves join the twigs, the tree seals over the junction and pushes off the leaves.

When the leaves fall off the tree they are dead, no longer receiving any food. Next year's leaf buds are already there on the tree, tightly rolled. In the spring, as the weather warms and the sap rises, they unfurl and the tree is green again.

WHEN I YAWN, WHY DO PEOPLE NEAR ME YAWN TOO?

ASKED BY Alex, age 7

Dr Jack Lewis, *neuroscientist and broadcaster, says:*

You yawn when your brain becomes a little bit hotter than it needs to be to work well. Yawning helps cool down the blood on its way up into your brain. This helps you to feel more alert and to focus your attention better when you're feeling sleepy. It fights the tiredness.

It often happens after you've been sitting around not doing very much, at the moment you realise it is time to do something more active. For instance, paratroopers often yawn just before they jump out of an aeroplane into enemy territory. I often yawn just before I go up on stage to give a talk to hundreds of people.

The reason that yawning is 'catching' or 'contagious' – other people near you yawn when you yawn – is to get everyone in the group ready to be more active. When other people 'catch' your yawn, their brain gets cooled down as well. This gets everyone more alert and focused *at the same time.*

Riot policemen often yawn together just before they go in to break up a fight, usually when they have waited around for ages before the order to move is given. For the rest of us, catching someone else's yawn prepares us for a much less exciting activity – getting everyone ready to get up and go to bed at the same time!

WHY ARE QUENTIN BLAKE'S DRAWINGS SO MESSY?

ASKED BY Hal, age 8

Sir Quentin Blake, *artist, says:*

Greetings! Good is not the same as neat. My drawings don't look so messy to me because by the time I have finished, the lines are exactly where I want them to be. Even if they don't join up. And if the lines don't quite join up and the colour does not fit in a tidy way, that is because I am often drawing something happening, and I want to suggest it hasn't quite finished yet.

WHY DO BABOONS HAVE RED BUMS?

ASKED BY Jarae, age 9

Kate Humble, *wildlife TV presenter, says:*

Girls sometimes go to enormous efforts to be
noticed by boys. They might spend hours choosing
the right clothes and shoes, doing their hair, putting
on make-up. But boys can be staggeringly unob-
servant at times. My mum once dyed her hair pink
to see if my dad would notice. He didn't. And it's
not just human males that sometimes need a not-so-
subtle hint that a girl might be interested in them.
Baboons need it too.

Baboons live in troops – big, extended families
of males, females and youngsters. The males have
a lot to do. They have to find food, groom themselves to make sure they are free of nasty parasites,
help look after the younger members of the troop,
keep watch for things like leopards that like to eat
baboons, and fight each other to prove which one of
them is the strongest.

Like us, female baboons want a mate that is big,

strong, healthy and fit. Since male baboons have so many other things to think about, female baboons have had to develop a very obvious way of letting the males know when they are ready to mate. They don't send a text, or organise a romantic dinner for two. Instead, their bottoms swell up and turn bright red. And clearly it works, because baboons are the most widespread primate in Africa.

WHAT DID WINSTON CHURCHILL DO FOR BRITAIN?

ASKED BY Sienna, age 6

Dan Snow, *historian, says:*

Winston Churchill was not a particularly good soldier, nor was he a perfect leader. He often made mistakes and took the wrong decision. He was not even a brilliant politician: he made enemies easily and lots of other politicians did not really trust him. But Winston Churchill got one thing absolutely right, and it was one of the best things anyone in Britain has ever done, with people around the whole world still benefiting from it today.

In the summer of 1940 when it looked like Hitler's Germany had won the Second World War, and lots of people were calling on Churchill to give up and make peace with Hitler, he insisted, absolutely insisted, on fighting on. He understood what we all know now, that the Nazis were a 'monstrous tyranny', more evil and destructive than any of the other terrible empires, countries and people in history.

Years later, when it emerged that Hitler had murdered millions and millions of Jews, Poles, Russians and anyone else who disagreed with him, Churchill was proved right. Through a series of inspiring speeches, Churchill convinced Britain, and the world, that the war was not just a squabble for power between countries, like so many wars before, but a unique struggle for civilisation and the future of the world.

WHAT IS THE DIFFERENCE BETWEEN A METEOR AND AN ASTEROID?

ASKED BY Harry, age 9

Andrea Wulf, *author of books about science and nature, says:*

Think of an asteroid as a big chunk of rock going around the Sun. They are not as big as planets but they can be quite enormous, like the one called Ceres which is nearly 1,000 kilometres across – that's more than the distance from Paris to Berlin. There are millions of asteroids in our solar system.

If an asteroid enters our Earth's atmosphere, it becomes a meteor. That's probably the reason why people sometimes get confused about which is which – because in a way it's still the same object. Once the asteroid – now called the meteor – hits our atmosphere it often burns up. Have you ever seen shooting stars? Those tails of white light in the night sky that flash up very quickly and then disappear? That's a meteor burning up.

And to make it even more confusing . . . if a meteor manages to fall through our atmosphere without burning up but actually crashes onto Earth (onto the ground or into the ocean) it becomes a meteorite.

WHY CAN'T CARS RUN ON SOMETHING OTHER THAN PETROL, LIKE WATER?

ASKED BY Jonty, age 9

Quentin Cooper, *science and arts broadcaster and writer, says:*

Motoring has never been purely for petrolheads. Right from the start, well over a century ago, many drivers had electric automobiles, and even the first affordable mass-produced car – Henry Ford's 1908 Model T Ford – was designed to run off ethanol as well as petrol.

Today there are tens of millions of alternative and flexible fuel vehicles on the road worldwide, between them able to run off anything from gas or biodiesel or electricity to – at least in a few cases – weirder things like hydrogen or solar power or even human waste. Yeuch!

Almost anything that can be an energy source can be used to power a vehicle. But not water. At least, not yet. Although many have claimed to have developed water-fuelled cars, in all cases (that I'm aware of) it has turned out to be an exaggeration, utterly impractical, or outright deception.

WHY DO ONIONS MAKE US CRY?

ASKED BY Matthew, age 9, and Eleanor, age 5

Greg Foot, *daredevil scientist, says:*

I don't know about you but I cry like a baby when I cut an onion! I can't help it – it's all down to chemistry.

Slicing through an onion with your knife rips open its cells, releasing various chemicals that react together. After about thirty seconds (notice how you don't cry straight away?) a sulphur-carrying gas is produced that wafts up to your eye. It mixes with the water in your eye, producing a burning sulphuric acid. That's what causes the discomfort.

But what about the tears? Well, the front of your eyeball – your cornea – is packed with nerve endings to detect any physical or chemical irritants. They sense that tear-provoking chemical and send a signal to your tear glands to boost the production of tears to flush it away. So you're left crying into your bolognaise sauce.

How can you spare yourself the blubbing? Cut the onion under water to soak up that irritating chemical, chill it in the fridge first to slow down those reactions, or wear goggles and a snorkel!

WHY DO ZEBRAS HAVE STRIPES?

ASKED BY Rachel, age 8, and Thulani, age 7

Dr Karen James, *biologist, says:*

When we want to understand why a plant or animal is the way it is, we start by asking three questions: 1) Is it that way because it helps them to survive or to have offspring, or just 'by accident'? 2) If it does help, how might it help? 3) Is there any evidence that this is how it helps?

Starting with question 1, how could you tell if zebras are helped by their stripes? Maybe you could find a herd of zebras, paint a third of them solid white, a third solid black, and leave a third unpainted, then see how many survive and successfully raise another generation of zebras. The thing is . . . have you ever tried to catch and paint a zebra? Me neither, but it sounds tricky!

Moving on to question 2, even if we're not sure the stripes help zebras, we can still ask, 'How *might* they help?' Some scientists think stripes camouflage zebras in tall grass. Others think stripes make it difficult for predators like lions to single a zebra out from the herd; where does one zebra end and another begin? Another idea is that zebras might use their unique stripe patterns to identify each other, the way we use faces.

It's nice to have ideas, but now we have to move on to question 3, 'Is there any evidence?' If we read the scientific literature, we find the answer for all these ideas is 'no'. But there is another idea . . .

In addition to big predators, like lions, there are small predators that can hurt zebras: biting flies. They carry diseases and distract zebras from feeding and watching for the bigger predators.

In 2011, scientists set wooden models of zebras out in a field. Some of the models were painted with stripes, some were solid white, some solid black. Sound familiar? Next they painted the models with sticky glue. They found that the solid black models 'caught' the most biting flies, the solid white models caught fewer, and the zebra-striped models caught the least of all.

At last, some evidence: zebras' stripes might repel biting flies, like a visual bug spray!

WHO INVENTED BALLOONS?

ASKED BY Amal, age 10

John and Mary Gribbin, *authors of science books, say:*

Rubber balloons were invented in 1824 by a famous scientist, Michael Faraday. He was doing experiments with hydrogen gas, but he didn't have anywhere to keep the gas. So he got two sheets of rubber, put one on top of the other and squeezed the edges hard in a machine to make them stick together. The middle of the rubber was covered in flour to stop it sticking, and there was a gap in one end to let the hydrogen gas in. Because hydrogen is lighter than air, the balloons full of hydrogen would float in the air.

This was such good fun that just a year later, a toy maker called Thomas Hancock started selling kits for people to make their own balloons to play with. But hydrogen can catch fire and burn very fiercely, so these days our balloons are filled with helium, which is also very light but doesn't burn. If you blow up a balloon with air, it won't float, but it is still fun to play with.

WHY DON'T OLD PEOPLE LIKE POP MUSIC?

ASKED BY Sasha, age 9

Ann Widdecombe, *novelist and former politician, says:*

Of course we like pop music, but the music we like was pop a long time ago. We object less to your music than to the volume at which you play it. It hurts our poor old ears and we can't hear ourselves speak because we no longer hear as well as when we were young – and ruining our own ears with loud pop music.

WHY DOES SWEETCORN COME OUT LOOKING THE SAME AS WHEN I ATE IT?

ASKED BY Keane, age 7, and Jules, age 6

Mary Roach, *author, says:*

A kernel of corn has a tough, fibrous 'seed coat' that stands up to the acids and digestive juices in your stomach – much the way a leather jacket protects a motorcycle rider. Corn is famous for its ability to pass through the body intact, or at least in recognisable pieces. For this reason, it can be used as a 'marker food' to measure how long it takes food to travel all the way through you.

The next time your family eats corn on the cob, you can do an experiment. Make a note of the date and time when you eat the corn, and then again when you next catch sight of it. The number of hours in between is the 'transit time' for your own intestines. (Some people might object to looking into the toilet, but based on your question, you won't have a problem. You have a healthy curiosity, and that's great!)

If you chew your corn thoroughly and break open

the seed coat, your body should be able to absorb the good nutrients inside. Birds don't have molars to break open seeds, so they poop them out whole, and then the seeds sprout where they land. Plants don't have legs or cars, so this is one way they get around. The pooping birds help the plants populate the far corners of the land.

The seeds of the baobab tree, on the African savannah, are so tough that chimps can't chew them up. So they eat them twice. They pluck the undissolved (but softened) seeds out of their poop and run them through their digesting machinery again. The second time around, the seeds break apart. You'll be happy to learn that when the chimps are done, they wipe their lips with tree bark.

WHERE DOES COUNTING COME FROM?

ASKED BY Tommy, age 7

Alex Bellos, *maths author, says:*

Probably from gazing at the Moon. Our ancient ancestors will have noticed that the Moon follows a cycle, from Full Moon to New Moon and then back again.

In order to track the position of the Moon on its cycle, our ancestors would have made notches on pieces of wood or bone, or painted splotches on rock walls, to mark the days as they passed. Each notch or splotch represented a day, a bit like the way a prisoner in a film marks a line on the wall of his cell every day, in order to remember how long he has been there.

The purpose of counting therefore stemmed from the human desire to track time, which thousands of years later led to the invention of numbers.

WHY DOESN'T THE MONA LISA HAVE EYEBROWS?

ASKED BY Maia, age 11

Professor Martin Kemp, *expert on Leonardo da Vinci, says:*

A surprisingly difficult question! Either they have been cleaned off or they were never there. I suspect the former. Very slight eyebrows, presumably plucked until they were extremely thin, can be seen on some of the better early copies. Leonardo painted such details with incredibly fine and delicate touches of paint applied with a tiny brush. The little fringe of lace at the top of the neckline of her dress has gone. Lisa's eyebrows are likely to have suffered the same fate.

IN THE FUTURE WILL TELEPORTING EXIST?

ASKED BY Sebbie, age 9

Brian Clegg, *science author, says:*

It already does! But only on a very small scale. A clever bit of science called quantum teleportation lets us transmit an identical copy of an atom anywhere else we can send a special signal, and could work on something as big as a virus.

Some time in the future we might be able to do this with a person, but it would mean working on each atom separately – and you have so many atoms in your body, if it could look at a trillion of them a second the teleport machine would still take 200 million years to scan you.

The other problem is that it would work by making an exact copy that even had your thoughts and memories, but it would do this by ripping the original you to pieces. Everyone else would just see you appear at the far end, but it doesn't sound a fun way to travel.

We may never have teleporters for people, but quantum teleportation is already being used in special quantum computers that use the tiny building blocks of the Universe, like the photons that make up light, to do their calculations.

WHO KILLED THE LAST DODO?

ASKED BY Marc, age 12

Dr Julian Hume, *researcher at the Natural History Museum in London, says:*

Imagine you are a Dutch sailor. The date is September 1598. You have been at sea for months, the food on board is rotten and the water stagnant. Many of your friends are sick. A great storm has blown your ship hundreds of miles off course and you are lost at sea.

Suddenly, you spot an island. Exploring it with the rest of the crew, you find it is covered in forest, rich in palms and valuable ebony trees, and sweet fresh water runs down from the mountains. You have discovered the island of Mauritius.

Birds are everywhere on this island and so tame that they can be caught by hand. You notice that one bird stands out from the rest. It is as big as a turkey, with a large hooked bill and tiny wings. It's called a dodo. The dodo shows no fear of humans, so twenty of them are easily killed with sticks and loaded onto the ship. What a story to tell when you get home!

Within a year the news is out about the island and now many ships stop there to get food and water. Pigs, goats, monkeys and deer are released to provide extra food. Rats escape and breed in huge numbers. The ebony trees are cut down and the forests destroyed.

The dodo had lived for millions of years in peace and without competition, but now its home is besieged. Just eighty years later, somewhere in a remote part of the island, the last dodo passes away. The dodo is extinct.

DO ANIMALS LIKE COWS AND SHEEP HAVE ACCENTS?

ASKED BY Angelina, age 6

Professor John Wells, *phonetics expert, says:*

Unlike human beings, animals don't have languages. They do produce 'vocalisations' (dogs bark,
cats miaow, sheep bleat, cows moo, birds chirp),
but these are not language, even though they are a
means of communicating.

As you will know if you've ever watched sheep-
dog trials, we can teach dogs to understand quite
complicated spoken instructions. But they can't
speak to us. If you've been out, leaving your dog
in the house, you can't ask him when you get back,
'Did anyone phone while I was out?' and he can't
tell you, 'The phone did ring, but I didn't answer it.
And someone knocked at the door, too.'

Different breeds of dog may have different kinds
of bark, and you may even be able to recognise an
individual dog's bark just as you can an individual
person's voice. But a dog's bark does not depend on
where it grew up and who its friends are or where

66

it went to school – which are the main things that determine your accent or mine.

Scientists have found that whales in different oceans make different kinds of vocalisation, and the calls of some species of birds vary from one location to another. So we could perhaps say that whales and birds can have local 'accents' or 'dialects'. But domestic cows and sheep are different. Where they grow up and live is decided by the human beings that own them.

A few years ago newspapers carried a story saying that cows in Somerset moo with a distinctive West Country accent. But the story was untrue. It had been thought up to get publicity for a company selling cheese. As far as we know, Somerset cows moo in just the same way as cows in Yorkshire or Norfolk.

HOW DID IAN FLEMING MAKE UP JAMES BOND?

ASKED BY Fergus, age 9

William Boyd, *novelist and screenwriter, says:*

In the Second World War Ian Fleming was a British espionage officer who worked for an organisation called the Naval Intelligence Division. It was the time of his life when he was at his happiest. After the war, needing to make some money, he decided to write a spy novel and he invented a spy who could do all the things that he, Ian Fleming, had never been able to do. Through his novels he was able to live a kind of imaginary life of action and adventure and evil villains and beautiful women.

But he couldn't think of a name for this spy. He wanted something very simple and very British. One day at his desk he picked up a book on bird-watching (Ian Fleming was a very keen bird-watcher). This book was written by an ornithologist called James Bond. Ian Fleming decided to borrow the name for his fictional spy. And so James Bond was born!

68

CAN A ROBIN BE FRIENDS WITH A BLACKBIRD?

ASKED BY Polly, age 4

Bill Oddie, *birdwatcher and broadcaster, says:*

The honest truth is that robins have quite a lot of trouble being friends with each other! If there is a pair of robins in the garden and another one appears, the male will chase the new one away or there might be a fight, with beaks stabbing and feathers flying.

Last year, robins nested in my garden. They brought their kids up really attentively but once they were out of the nest and could fly, I often saw the mum or dad chasing their own offspring, or the fledglings scrapping with each other. Just to illustrate how aggressive robins can be, we once did an experiment putting a fake robin on a fence near a nest. The male robin knocked its head off!

As it happens, robins and blackbirds belong to the same family. They are both thrushes. Similar shape, similar beaks and they both eat worms. As long as there was enough food to go round, they probably wouldn't bother each other much but I don't think they'd qualify as friends.

What would be a bird's idea of friendship? Are birds that nest in large numbers in colonies friends or just neighbours? If there is such a thing as animal friendship between two different species, I suspect it is more likely in captivity or between pets. Think of those pictures in the papers of a kitten cuddling up to a pit bull or a budgie perched on a tortoise or . . . well, you have a go! A what with a what?

So a robin with a blackbird? I have never seen them cuddling, but I have just been in the garden putting out mealworms, and both robin and blackbird fed from my hand. I don't know how they feel about each other, but they are both friends to me.

COULD I SURVIVE ON JUST BANANAS?

ASKED BY Katie, age 9

Annabel Karmel, *parenting author, says:*

Bananas are a great food but no, you cannot survive by eating them only. A healthy diet means a good variety of foods. Eating any food just by itself would not be good for you, as you would only be getting a particular set of nutrients. So really you couldn't survive for a long time by eating only one type of food, whatever it was.

Eating bananas would probably keep you going for a while, as long as you were drinking plenty of liquids too. Bananas contain potassium, a micro-nutrient that we need in our diet, but we need it in balance with other minerals. Too much potassium can be toxic and can cause problems with our nerves and heart.

Bananas contain around 0.4 grams of potassium, and the recommended amount of potassium for four-to eight-year-olds is 3.8 grams a day. So even if you ate ten bananas a day you would be eating just over your recommended daily amount, but you wouldn't have a toxic amount of potassium in your body. Ten bananas in one day would be a lot of bananas to eat: you would probably be bored of the taste of them, and you might also have a bit of a sore tummy and be visiting the loo a lot as bananas contain a lot of fibre!

WHY DO AMAZING BOOKS MAKE YOU CRY?

ASKED BY Jimmy, age 10

Jojo Moyes, *author, says:*

With the best books, you are pulled into them as if you were experiencing the same things the characters are going through. In my favourite books I have raced a horse, run terrified from a bad guy, and wept at the death of someone I cared about (even if they did only exist on a page!).

If I cry at a book, it's because the characters have become real to me, and I feel as sad about bad things happening to them as I would if it was someone in real life. I cried at the end of *Charlotte's Web* – even though I don't really like spiders. When Aslan from *The Lion, the Witch and the Wardrobe* made his brave sacrifice I cried too.

Even grown-ups do it. I cried last week at John Green's *The Fault in Our Stars*. So I'm delighted when people say that they have cried at my books: it means I have created something real, and someone that readers care about.

WHY DOES THE TIDE GO IN AND OUT?

ASKED BY Leon, age 6

John and Mary Gribbin, *authors of science books, say:*

Tides go in and out because the water in the sea is being pulled by the Sun and Moon. This pull is called gravity, and it is the same as the pull of the Earth that holds us down on the ground and gives us weight. (Weight is the pull of the Earth on something.)

Everything pulls on everything else by gravity. But the pull is bigger for bigger things, and less for things that are farther away. Even though the Sun is bigger than the Moon, it is much farther away, so its effect on tides is only about half as big as the effect of the Moon.

The pattern of tides is complicated because the Moon is going round the Earth, the Earth is going round the Sun, and the Earth is turning round once a day. But one pattern stands out. When the Sun and Moon are nearly in a line, around New Moon

74

and Full Moon, the Sun effect and the Moon effect add together and we have very high 'spring' tides. They get their name because they spring up very high. But near half Moon, the Sun effect and Moon effect partly cancel out, and even the high tides are not particularly high. They are called 'neap' tides.

Tides don't just affect the sea. They pull on the Earth's crust too. Depending on where on Earth you live, the whole solid ground goes up and down by as much as half a metre each day, carrying you with it!

WHICH DINOSAUR WAS THE FIRST ON EARTH?

ASKED BY Phyllis, age 9

Dr Paul Barrett, *dinosaur expert, says:*

The discovery of the earliest known dinosaur was announced in 2013. It is called *Nyasasaurus* (nye-ahsa-sore-us) and it lived in what is now Tanzania, in East Africa. It was a small animal, only one to two metres in length, and probably walked upright on its hind legs.

The rocks containing the bones of *Nyasasaurus* come from a period of time called the Middle Triassic and are around 245 million years old. This is about 15 million years older than other early dinosaur fossils.

Unfortunately, we don't know what *Nyasasaurus* ate, as the available fossils are missing teeth and claws, which are those parts of the skeleton that give us the best clues to an animal's diet. In fact, only two skeletons are known at the moment: one that has only some of the bones of the neck and another that has an arm bone and a number of back bones.

Bones of *Nyasasaurus* are very rare, which is not surprising as they are from the very early beginnings of the dinosaur group. *Nyasasaurus* lived in a world that was dominated by other sorts of reptile, in particular those related to today's crocodiles, and another group called the synapsids (sigh-nap-sids) that are the early ancestors of our own group, the mammals.

WHY DO STARS TWINKLE?

ASKED BY James, age 7

Dr Heather Couper, *astrophysicist, says:*

'Twinkle, twinkle, little star. How I wonder what you are?' But why do they twinkle? First – stars are not 'little'! They're huge balls of hot gas, many millions of kilometres across, like our local star, the Sun. It's only their vast distances from us that make them seem 'little'. And the twinkling has nothing to do with the star – it's all to do with Earth's atmosphere.

Imagine floating in a swimming pool and gazing up at your surroundings as the water tumbles over you. It's all blurry. And that's true when you look through our shifting atmosphere at the remote stars. Warm and cold currents of air are washing above you, making them fade and flash. Twinkling is most spectacular when a star is near the horizon – that's where you're looking through the greatest thickness of air.

Planets *don't* twinkle, which is how you can tell a planet from a star in the sky. Because the planets in our solar system are so much closer than the stars

– which just look like points of light – they appear bigger, and the atmosphere doesn't distort them in the same way.

WHAT DO NEWSPAPERS DO WHEN THERE'S NO NEWS?

ASKED BY Hannah, age 8

Oliver Burkeman, *journalist, says:*

Some of the very earliest newspapers weren't published at regular intervals: they only came out when there were events worth reporting. But the truth is that there's always news. After all, 'news' just means something that's new – something you haven't heard of before.

So a good reporter can always find something to fill the space: there are millions of things going on in the world, and only a few pages in a newspaper. Do you know what daily life is like for someone working in a Chinese factory making laptop computers? If not, then for you an article about that counts as news.

Then there are investigative reporters, who spend weeks or months unearthing a crime or a political scandal: they're making the news, not just reporting on an event. Paparazzi photographers who lie in wait for Lady Gaga are making the news, too, whether or not you approve of what they're doing.

This all goes to show that newspapers don't really go out and *find* the news: they *decide* what gets to count as news. The same goes for television and radio. And you might disagree with their decisions! (For example, journalists are often accused of focusing on bad news and ignoring the good, making the world seem worse than it is.)

The important thing to remember, whenever you're reading or watching the news, is that someone decided to tell you those things, while leaving out other things. They're presenting one particular view of the world – not the only one. There's always another side to the story.

WHY DON'T GIRL LIONS HAVE MANES?

ASKED BY Grace, age 7

Simon King, *wildlife film-maker and naturalist, says:*

Male lions have manes for a variety of reasons. One is to advertise the fact that they are in charge of a territory or are intending to take over a new one – their manes can be seen from a great distance, alerting rivals to their presence. The mane also helps protect the lion's face and neck when fighting over territory.

The biggest and most dramatic black manes are found on the lions within the Masai Mara wildlife reserve in Kenya.

As female lions – or lionesses – are less likely to fight for territory and instead spend most of their time hunting for food, they don't want to be so noticeable, so having no mane helps them keep a low profile.

WHEN WERE PANTOMIMES INVENTED?

ASKED BY Eloise, age 9

Dr Bettany Hughes, *historian, says:*

You can be a detective when it comes to the history of anything. Like many lovely English words 'pantomime' is pretty much pure Ancient Greek. It comes from *pantos* meaning 'all' and *mimos* meaning 'actor'. So pantomime actors in Ancient Greece and Rome used to put on shows for their mates.

In Britain, in medieval times or even earlier, we started to have crazy festivals to let off a bit of steam, where the 'world was turned upside down'. Men dressed as women, poor people as kings . . . stuff like that. But it wasn't until around 1720 that Drury Lane Theatre in London experimented with the first proper pantomime: dancing and slapstick jokes were added to a famous plot. Actually this wasn't a big success but thank goodness we stuck with the idea! I have always adored pantomimes.

My lovely actor dad often played the dame at Richmond Theatre – every year my Santa stocking was his old, traditional red-and-white stripy stocking from the dame's pantomime costume!

WHAT IS THE WHOLE POINT OF SCIENCE?

ASKED BY Louise, age 7

Sir John Gurdon, *Nobel Prize-winning biologist, says:*

Science makes continuous advances in the quality of human life.

WHY DO SCORPIONS GLOW UNDER ULTRAVIOLET LIGHT?

ASKED BY Shirin, age 8

Dr Douglas D. Gaffin, *biologist, says:*

You have asked a tough question. An easier one would be: '*How* do scorpions glow under ultraviolet light?' The glow comes from a couple of chemicals in their skin that react when ultraviolet (UV) light hits them. UV light, which we cannot see, causes tiny particles called electrons in these chemicals to get excited. When the electrons relax, they let off the green light that we can see.

But you asked 'why'. Well, lots of people have suggested possible answers, but no one is quite sure. One idea is that the glow from female scorpions attracts male scorpions. A second is that they may be attracting a meal. Scorpions come out at night and hunt moths and other insects. These bugs are attracted to light and may be lured to the hungry scorpion's faint glow.

A third idea is that scorpions use their skin to 'feel' dim light. Mice and owls eat scorpions, which means that scorpions must sometimes run and hide. If a scorpion can feel starlight with its skin, then it might find a safe place by running until any part of its body is shaded. Perhaps they glow because their senses are best at detecting green light. By absorbing starlight and giving off green light, the skin gives the animal the best chance of finding shade.

There are other possible answers to your question as well, including the possibility that their glow has no function at all – other than to inspire great students like you to notice, ask questions and think about the possibilities.

WHY DOESN'T MY DADDY EVER WIN THE LOTTERY?

ASKED BY Connie, age 5

Tim Harford, *Undercover Economist, says:*

There are forty-nine lottery balls, and to win the lottery your dad needs to pick the same six that emerge from the lottery draw. That sounds hard. In fact, it's much, much harder than you think. The chance of picking the first ball correctly is one in forty-nine (1/49). Then, because your dad already got the first ball, the chance of picking the second ball correctly is 1/48. The third one is 1/47. And so on. Multiply all those numbers together and you get a tiny, tiny chance: one in 10 billion(ish).

Actually your dad's chances are better than that, because if he gets the right six balls, he is allowed to have them in any order. There are 720 different possible ways to arrange six balls, and any one of them wins. So your dad's chance of winning the lottery is not one in 10 billion(ish) but 720 in 10 billion(ish) – or about one in 14 million. One in 14 million is a very small chance of winning. It's not a clever game to play.

The truth is that people are far more likely to keel over dead than win the lottery. There are 56 million people in England and Wales, which is exactly four times 14 million. If everyone bought one ticket every week, you'd expect four winners. But compare those four winners to the 10,000 people in England and Wales who die every week. If someone buys a lottery ticket at the beginning of the week, they are 2,500 times more likely to die that week than they are to win.

WHY DO GIRLS LIKE DOLLS AND BOYS LIKE CARS?

ASKED BY Charlie, age 9

Professor Simon Baron-Cohen,
psychologist, says:

It's not that all girls like dolls – there are plenty of girls who are completely bored by dolls – and it's not that all boys like cars – there are plenty of boys who are completely bored by cars. But if you leave toys out on the carpet and film how long children play with each of these two types of toys, more girls than boys play with dolls and more boys than girls play with toy cars.

This could be because their parents, or other adults, have encouraged them to play with one type of toy or the other, or because they've watched other children of the same sex playing with one kind of toy or the other. My own view is that this is only part of the answer. It doesn't completely explain it.

One study found that newborn baby boys look longer at mechanical objects, and newborn baby girls look longer at faces, and these differences are happening before adults or other children have had a chance to influence what babies are interested in. If these differences in interests can be seen at birth it means that a person's *biology*, before birth (such as their hormones or genes), must be part of the explanation.

A clue that hormones are involved comes from studies of babies followed up from pregnancy, when the so-called 'male hormone', testosterone, is measured in the fluid around the baby. (Both male and female babies produce testosterone while in the womb, but males produce much more of it.) How much testosterone a baby produces predicts their patterns of behaviour (e.g. how much they look at faces) after they are born.

So social experience is important, but so is biology.

WHAT MAKES WAVES IN THE OCEAN?

ASKED BY Alice, age 11

Dr Helen Czerski, *physicist, says:*

You can start a wave yourself, next time you have a hot drink. Gently blow sideways across the top of the liquid (just as you would to cool it down). You'll see ripples starting on one side and travelling across to the other. The air you blow pushes the surface along, and so waves grow.

Now imagine that you could keep blowing (you'd need very large lungs!) for miles and miles . . . the waves would just get bigger and bigger. And this is what happens on the ocean. The wind pushes on the water, and waves grow. Because the ocean is so big, and winds push on the water for hundreds of miles, the waves can get really huge. If they get big enough, they break, and you get lots of bubbles and foam. That's the end of the wave.

If they don't break, the waves keep travelling across the ocean, sometimes for thousands of miles. When they arrive at the seaside, they have to break as the water gets shallower. So a breaking wave at the shore is the end of a wave that could have been made days ago, far away across the ocean.

DOES MY GOLDFISH KNOW WHO I AM?

ASKED BY Shauna, age 10

Dr Mike Webster, *biologist, says:*

I think this is a great question, but then I do spend my days studying how fish go about their lives. First of all, fish are much smarter than people give them credit for. People often talk of goldfish having three-second memories, but actually they can learn all kinds of things, and remember them for quite a long time.

This shouldn't surprise us too much. Just like other animals, they have evolved to find enough to eat, and to know when it is safe to be out in the open. Being able to learn and remember things helps them do this.

Many kinds of fish can tell each other apart, too. They recognise other fish from their shoal, their relatives, and even their own eggs. But fish live in a very different world from us. For many kinds of fish, although seeing is important, senses such as smell and touch are even more important.

So, does your fish know who you are? I'm sure your fish will certainly know when it is feeding time. My own fish become very excited when I open up the lid on their tank and my hand appears, even before I drop the food in. I'm not sure that your fish would be able to remember what your face looks like, but I wouldn't be too surprised if it could rec-ognise you in other ways, perhaps by the sound of your footsteps as you walk towards the tank.

HOW DID CLOCKS GET INVENTED?

ASKED BY Aimée, age 9

Adam Hart-Davis, *author and former broadcaster, says:*

People have always lived by the Sun, getting up after sunrise and going to bed after sunset, and eating their lunch when they felt hungry in the middle of the day. Some ancient people wanted to ask their friends round at a particular time; so they divided the day (sunrise to sunset) into twelve hours.

They used sundials to measure the daylight hours, but sundials don't work at night, so what they came up with was the water clock. The Greek *klepsydra*, or 'water thief', was basically a pot with a small hole in the bottom. The water inside would steadily run out, so when they looked at how much water had gone they could work out how much time had passed.

In about 1580 the Italian scientist Galileo saw the great bronze lamp swinging in the cathedral at Pisa, realised that a pendulum swings in a regular way, and suggested that it would be a good basis for a clock. He found that a pendulum one metre long takes almost exactly one second to swing from left to right, regardless of how far it swings. The first pendulum clock was built in 1657 by the Dutch scientist Christian Huygens, and pendulum clocks have been running ever since.

Most of today's clocks and watches use tiny quartz crystals as regulators. When it is connnected to a battery, the quartz vibrates exactly 32,768 times a second, and a counter moves the second hand on every 32,768 vibrations.

WHY DO YOU CLOSE YOUR EYES WHEN YOU SNEEZE?

ASKED BY Leah, age 6

Dr Dawn Harper, *GP and broadcaster, says:*

When something makes the inside of your nose feel ticklish, a message is sent to the sneeze centre in your brain. The brain then sends a message to all the muscles that need to work to make you sneeze, and there are lots of them, more than fifty!

When you sneeze, muscles in your tummy, your chest, your throat and your eyelids all work together to get rid of whatever it is that's irritated your nose. You can't help it. It is impossible to sneeze without closing your eyes because that is what your brain says must happen. It's an automatic reflex – probably to protect the eyes from germs that might be sneezed out, but I don't think we know for sure.

Did you know that when you sneeze, tiny particles in your nose fly out at 100 miles an hour?

IF I HELD ENOUGH BALLOONS, COULD I LIFT OFF THE GROUND?

ASKED BY Benjamin, age 7

Jonathan R. Trappe, *cluster balloonist,** *says:*

Yes. If you had enough helium-filled balloons, you could float off the ground – and more. You could actually fly to tremendous altitudes, in the open blue skies, in complete silence, if you just had enough balloons. Now, your arms would get tired, so it might be better if you used some sort of a chair, harness or gondola to carry you; you could attach the helium balloons to that. It would be easier if you used pretty big balloons; it would take so many small ones.

Before your flight, I think you should first become a pilot and study how to read the winds. That way you could harness your knowledge and ride those winds, allowing them to carry you to destinations unknown at launch. What adventures you could

*Jonathan holds the world record for longest flight by helium balloons. Read about his flights on page 304.

99

have, in the open sky, in the open air, in the big blue, travelling the world using only wind, helium and hope.

HOW DOES MY BRAIN STORE LOTS OF INFORMATION WHEN IT'S ONLY SMALL?

ASKED BY Tom, age 9

Joshua Foer, *science journalist, says:*

An adult's brain only weighs about 1.4 kilograms, but it's made up of about 100 billion microscopic neurons. Each of those neurons looks like a tiny branching tree, whose limbs reach out and touch other neurons. In fact, each neuron can make between 5,000 and 10,000 connections with other neurons – sometimes even more. That's more than 500 trillion connections! A memory is essentially a pattern of connections between neurons.

Every sensation that you remember, every thought that you think, transforms your brain by altering the connections within that vast network. By the time you get to the end of this sentence, you will have created a new memory, which means your brain will have physically changed.

WHICH ANIMALS HAVE BEEN INTO SPACE?

ASKED BY Tyler, age 9

Jenny Marder, *science journalist, says:*

In 1946, scientists first launched a balloon into the Earth's upper atmosphere to study the effects of radiation on fruit flies. Since that time, rhesus monkeys, chimpanzees, dogs and rabbits have blasted off into space aboard rockets. So have mice, turtles, fish, jellyfish, algae, countless insects and thousands of worms.

By the time humans arrived in space, animals had already tested a living creature's ability to withstand radiation, weightlessness and motion sickness. They were the first real space pioneers.

Among them was Nefertiti or 'Nefi', a courageous spider who soared into orbit on 21 July 2012 aboard a Japanese HTV spacecraft and spent three months hunting fruit flies aboard the International Space Station before returning to Earth. She flew nearly 67 million kilometres during her outer space mission, and she adapted splendidly to zero gravity, researchers say.

Nefi was the size of a pencil eraser and black with a bright red spot on her abdomen. She had two large, forward-facing eyes which gave her excellent depth perception for stalking her prey. She was a jumping spider, which meant she hunted like a lion by leaping into the air, grabbing her prey with her front legs and digging into it with her fangs, injecting venom. She liked fruit flies, but preferred crickets.

In space, in microgravity, her behaviour changed. She sidled up to her prey instead of leaping onto it. And, interestingly, she produced more silk in her space habitat, which she may have used to anchor herself while weightless.

Back on Earth, she retired to the insect zoo at the Smithsonian Museum of Natural History in Washington DC. On 3 December 2012, the zoo manager awoke to a sad text message: 'Sorry, but we think Nefi is dead.' Nefertiti had indeed died. She was ten months old. On Thursday, she was eating crickets and her colour looked good. By Sunday, she was gone. The lifetime of her species, *Phidippus johnsoni*, is about a year.

Farewell, little space spider. You did well.

WHY DID THE ROMANS ALWAYS INVADE PLACES?

ASKED BY Katie, age 9

Tom Holland, *historian and author, says:*

The Romans kept invading places because they were very good at it. In fact, the more they did it, the better they became. This was because when they'd conquered people, they would generally invite them to become allies of Rome – like asking them to be on the same team.

In time, these allies would end up Roman themselves. First the people of the cities near to Rome became Romans; then all the Italians; then other people in the world beyond Italy. This meant that the Romans, who had begun their history as the citizens of a tiny city, ended up numbering millions. The more men they had, the more places they could invade; the more places they invaded, the more men they got.

No wonder that eventually the Roman Empire grew to become the largest in the world!

WHY DO OLD PEOPLE GET WRINKLES?

ASKED BY Aaminah, age 9, and Skye Kyra, age 8

Dr Max Pemberton, *doctor and author, says:*

Skin is elastic, a bit like a rubber band. This is because it contains something called collagen. When we smile or frown, the muscles under our skin contract to make the expression. This causes creases in our skin, but the skin bounces back into shape when the muscles relax, thanks to the collagen.

As we get older, the amount of collagen in our skin decreases, so it doesn't bounce back as well. Over time, lines develop where the skin has been creased. These are wrinkles.

Some people don't like getting wrinkles because they think it makes them look old, but I think they're interesting because every wrinkle tells a story. Every joke you have heard or every time you've been tickled slowly etches itself into your face. Someone with lots of wrinkles has had an interesting life. You can tell when an old person is fun to be around because they will have wrinkles in the corners of their eyes, which are made from laughing.

My mum has lots of wrinkles and she says I caused them because I was quite naughty at school and made her frown a lot. Next time you look at your mum or dad's face, look closely at their wrinkles. Ask them which ones you caused.

WHAT MADE HESTON BLUMENTHAL WANT TO BE A CHEF?

ASKED BY Luka, age 11

Heston Blumenthal, *chef, says:*

When I was sixteen, my mum and dad took my sister and me to a restaurant in Provence, in France. The restaurant had three Michelin stars, which is the highest award in the world for cooking, so the food was good of course – roast lamb carved at the table; soufflé with lobster sauce. But it wasn't just the food that hit me, it was the whole experience. The smell of lavender in the air. The chirrup of insects in the grass. The warmth of the sun on your face.

It was like a show for all the senses at once – sight, sound, smell, taste and touch – and I suddenly knew that I wanted to put on that kind of show. I wanted to cook food that was not only delicious but also stirred your emotions – that made you laugh, or made you think, or moved you in some way.

It took more than ten years of hard work (and lots of practice) to open my first restaurant but, since then, that's the kind of food I've been trying to put on the table.

WHY ARE FARTS FLAMMABLE?

ASKED BY Luke, age 9

Greg Foot, *daredevil scientist, says:*

Ha! I love this question. A fart is simply gas that builds up in your intestines and then escapes out of your bottom. Some can be 'silent and deadly' whereas others can sound like an elephant – the fart noise comes from your sphincter muscles vibrating when you shoot the gas out!

A fart is made up of different gases. Some is air that you swallow – mainly nitrogen by the time it reaches your intestines. Other gases like hydrogen, methane and carbon dioxide are produced by the friendly bacteria in your gut as they digest sugars in your food. It's this hydrogen and methane that make farts flammable. Apparently, farts burn with a yellow or blue flame (although blue is pretty rare). Don't try it though – I know someone who did and they got burnt *really* badly.

Bonus fact: Smelly farts stink if there is sulphur in those gases. Sulphur-rich foods like eggs and meat produce really gross farts!

WHY DO SOME FOOTBALLERS GET MORE MONEY THAN OTHERS, EVEN THOUGH THEY DON'T SCORE?

ASKED BY Ismail, age 10

Simon Kuper, *journalist, says:*

Perhaps the non-scoring players deserve even more money than they are getting. You can help your team in all sorts of ways without scoring. A good goalkeeper or defender is probably worth as much to a team as a good striker, even though keepers and defenders don't get half as many headlines.

Goalkeeper Petr Čech surely did as much as forward Didier Drogba to win Chelsea the Champions League in 2012 – but Drogba was made the hero. Probably too much money is paid to the guys who score goals. Forwards tend to earn more than goalkeepers (who are usually the worst paid players on the pitch). That is not fair.

In football, people talk too much about the player who puts the ball in the back of the net and not enough about all the teammates who made the goal possible.

WHY DO BUTTERFLIES FLY LIKE THEY DON'T KNOW WHERE THEY'RE GOING?

ASKED BY Steven, age 4

Patrick Barkham, *nature writer, says:*

Butterflies may flutter and dart about as if they are confused but they know where they are going more often than people do. When you see a butterfly flying close to the ground, weaving in and out of grasses and flowers, it is probably a female, searching for the right plant on which to lay its eggs.

When you see a butterfly flying along a hedgerow or around a garden flowerbed as if on patrol, it is most likely to be a male, looking for a female with which to mate.

If you see two butterflies spiral up into the air together, they are usually two males fighting: the winner will chase all butterflies – and other insects, such as bees – away from its territory.

Migrating butterflies, which fly into Britain across the sea from mainland Europe, take advantage of the wind and can fly at up to fifty kilometres per hour – twice their normal speed. Moths may blunder into you at night but butterflies rarely crash. In all my life watching butterflies, I've never had one bump into me.

HOW DEEP CAN A SUBMARINE GO?

ASKED BY Alex, age 10

James Nestor, *author of a book about deep sea exploration, says:*

Exactly 10,994 metres. Actually, submarines could go even deeper than that but the ocean floor won't let them. 10,994 metres is the absolute lowest point on Earth – that's deeper than the tallest mountain (Mount Everest) is high!

Only three people in history have made it down there. It wasn't easy. The pressures at the bottom of the ocean are over 1,000 times greater than they are up here on land. To put this in perspective, imagine balancing the Eiffel Tower on your big toe (ouch!) and then imagine hundreds of other Eiffel Towers balancing on every inch of your body (OUCH!). That's what it would feel like if you swam down 10,994 metres. (Honestly, you wouldn't make it past a couple of hundred metres without your head imploding, but that's another story.)

To survive these incredible pressures, submarines have to be built with steel, titanium or glass that is many centimetres thick so they won't be crushed to pieces. Interested in taking a ride way down deep? You're in luck. A company in Florida just announced plans to carry tourists to the deepest point on Earth in a big glass ball within the next couple of years, for about $50,000 a seat (about £32,000). Start saving up now, and remember: Don't hold your breath!

WHY CAN SOME PEOPLE SING BETTER THAN OTHERS?

ASKED BY Andrea, age 10

Gareth Malone, *choirmaster and singer, says:*

Life is quite unfair. Some people are born with elegant noses. Some people have perfect legs, which they can use to kick a ball into a goal from 100 paces. And some people have just the right amount of space inside their head and neck for sound to resonate, creating a beautiful voice.

But that's not the end of the story. Just having been born with the right instrument doesn't make you a great singer. It takes years of practice to learn the muscle control you need, and it takes years of listening to and studying music. And even with hard work you need a large dose of luck.

What makes a beautiful voice? It depends on who's listening.

Even if you think you can't sing, your voice may well be beautiful to your friends and family. So there's no reason not to try.

WHY DO MALE SEAHORSES HAVE THE BABIES?

ASKED BY Eleanor, age 7, and Jake, age 10

Dr Daphne Fairbairn, *evolutionary biologist, author and university professor, says:*

Male seahorses having babies may seem strange but it is really just a way that seahorses increase the chances that their babies will survive. Most female fish release their eggs and abandon them, leaving them to hatch on their own. The eggs are excellent food for many predators and almost all get eaten before they can hatch. Seahorses have evolved a strategy to protect their eggs.

The female deposits her eggs in a special pouch on the underside of the male's tail and the eggs develop there. The male keeps them safe within the pouch and even provides some nutrition for the eggs to help the developing embryos survive and grow. When the eggs hatch, contractions of the pouch help to push out the miniature seahorse babies so that they can swim away.

This fatherly care increases the chances of survival for the offspring and also frees the female to make another batch of eggs while her mate is nurturing the current batch. In this way, male pregnancy benefits both male and female seahorses by helping them to reproduce successfully in their dangerous environment.

DO CATS HAVE THE SAME GENES AS US?

ASKED BY Hailey, age 10

Sam Kean, *author of science books, says:*

Many of a cat's genes are almost exactly the same as ours, yes. But not all.

The ones that are pretty much the same are involved in basic biological processes, like breathing or sleeping or digesting food. In fact, these genes are quite similar in many animals, especially mammals. It's the genes for other things that are different. Cats don't speak a language like humans do, or walk on two feet. So cats don't have the genes that control those traits. Overall, the more human-like an animal is, the more genes it shares with us. Chimpanzees have over ninety-six per cent the same DNA as we do.

Because human beings are smarter than other animals and behave in more complicated ways, scientists once assumed that we had to have many more genes. Some scientists guessed we'd have 100,000 genes. It turns out that that isn't true. Humans have only around 23,000 genes – fewer than some grapes have!

But this told scientists something important. We may share a lot of genes with cats and chimpanzees (and even grapes), but our bodies *use* the genes in different ways. It's like a piano. All pianos have eighty-eight keys. But you can use the piano to play something very simple, like doh-re-mi, or something very complicated, like Beethoven. Human beings 'play' our DNA like Beethoven, and that's what makes us special creatures.

WHY DO MOSQUITOES ONLY BITE SOME PEOPLE?

ASKED BY Charlotte, age 8

Dr Rob Hicks, *GP, medical journalist and presenter, says:*

Mosquitoes have a really powerful sense of smell and are attracted to chemicals that we all release from our bodies. One of these is carbon dioxide, which is in the air we breathe out, and mosquitoes use it like a signpost to help them find a possible meal. Women, and large people, tend to breathe out more carbon dioxide, and the more carbon dioxide breathed out, the easier it is for the mosquito to find you.

Just like you might like some foods but not others, mosquitoes like some chemicals more than others. As the mosquito gets closer to someone it detects whether the combination of chemicals from the person's body means they'll be a tasty snack or not. It's sort of like a pizza – if you like cheese, tomato and sausage, and that's what's on the pizza, then you'll probably eat it. However, if the pizza has foods on it

119

that you don't like then you'll probably want to eat something else. So, if you produce the chemicals they like, the mosquitoes will head for you.

Now, some people also make chemicals that mosquitoes don't like. These can act like a shield so the mosquito stays away and flies off to bite someone else!

WHY IS NEW YORK CALLED THE BIG APPLE?

ASKED BY Ellen, age 10

Philip Gooden, *author of books about words, says:*

There's an old American expression 'to bet a big apple' and it means to be very certain of what you're talking about. Then about a hundred years ago the 'big apple' started to be applied to horse racing in New York, perhaps because it was the most important centre for horse races or because of the value of the prizes. From there the expression grew even wider until it came to describe the city itself, especially during an age when it was one of the most exciting, fast-moving and glamorous places on Earth.

After a time, advertisers started using the words and even the image of a large, glossy, unblemished apple because they realised it was a good way to encourage people to visit the city. It's true too: New York is like the biggest apple in the world, the shiny object that everybody wants a slice of.

HOW DO PEOPLE SQUIRT MILK OUT OF THEIR EYES?

ASKED BY Ben, age 10

Ilker Yilmaz, *champion milk squirter, says:*

I hold the world record for the longest jet of milk squirted from the eye. How do I do it? I breathe the milk in through my nose. Then I pinch my nostrils and blow (as if blowing my nose but still keeping my nostrils pinched). The pressure sends the milk up through my tear duct, the channel that leads from my nose to the inside corner of my eye. And out it squirts! My record is for squirting milk a distance of two metres, seventy-nine centimetres and five millimetres. The reason I can do this is my left tear duct is wider than most people's.

Everyone has tear ducts that lead from eye to nose. Inside, it's all connected. That's why, when you cry, your nose runs – some of the tears are draining from your eyes through your nose. If you look at your eyes in the mirror you'll see a dot in the inside corner of each eyelid, top and bottom. These are openings to your tear ducts.

A doctor will tell you it's not good to squirt milk out of your eye, so don't do it yourself. You could get an infection or damage your eye. Milk might end up in your ear. But I hope my answer has made you happy.

HOW COME PLANES DON'T CRASH IN THE SKY?

ASKED BY Phoebe, age 5

Brian Clegg, *author of science books, says:*

There are so many cars on the roads it's not surprising they have a lot of bumps – but there really aren't many planes in the sky at the same time, and they have much more space to fly around in. Planes that are close to each other have to be at least 300 metres apart in height, or five kilometres apart side to side if they're at the same height.

To be doubly sure, air traffic controllers keep an eye on where planes are going on their radar, keeping them on safe courses. Airliners also have radar for their pilots to use, and a special 'traffic alert and collision avoidance system' which automatically talks by radio with any nearby planes and makes sure they don't get too close. Military planes occasionally do crash because they often fly just metres away from each other – but they are the exception.

HOW DO WE LEARN TO SPEAK?

ASKED BY Ethan, age 7

Professor Gary Marcus, *cognitive scientist and author, says:*

All the best scientists and engineers at Google, Apple and Microsoft still haven't figured out how to build a machine that learns to talk as well as you do. Learning language is like breaking a code, and it's one of the most spectacular things that any human being ever does.

To learn to speak, the first thing that you have to do is discover the words in your language. What do they sound like? Every language is different. If you listen carefully to a foreign language, you will discover that it's sometimes hard to tell even what words other people are saying.

The second step is to learn what those words mean. Words for basic objects like *cup* and *ball* come relatively easily, because your parents can point to those things, but words like *nap* and *idea* are more complex, because you can't directly point to them.

The third step is to understand how to put those words together. The sentence 'The boy likes the girl' is different from the sentence 'The girl likes the boy', simply because the *order* of the words is different. It's a big deal when you figure that out!

The most amazing thing of all is that you figured out most of how language works without anyone telling you. Children are born with an instinct for learning language, just like birds are born with an instinct for learning to fly!

WHAT CAUSES FOOD POISONING?

ASKED BY Alice, age 11

Aggie MacKenzie, *Dirt Detective, says:*

Bacteria are everywhere. Most bacteria are harmless: they are all over our bodies, and we need them to keep us healthy and ward off disease.

Harmful bacteria such as campylobacter and E. coli live in our gut and poo, and should remain there! If they get into your stomach (by way of your mouth), you can become ill. For instance, if foods such as chicken or sausages are not cooked thoroughly, food-poisoning bacteria may not be killed off, and will multiply.

Bacteria may also multiply if fresh food has not been kept cold enough. If someone is ill or has not washed their hands properly after going to the loo and then they prepare food, the germs on their hands will be transferred to the food and then into your tummy and can make you ill. Food-poisoning symptoms are normally vomiting and diarrhoea.

The problem with bacteria is that you can't see the germs, and so you can easily forget they're there. The most important way of preventing food-poisoning germs harming you is for everyone to remember to wash their hands properly with warm water and soap, then dry them on a clean towel, both after visiting the loo and before eating or preparing food.

WHY ARE WHALES SO BIG?

ASKED BY Lara, age 10

Dr Yan Wong, *evolutionary scientist, says:*

Not everything can be big. A small cube of jelly keeps its shape. But one the size of a house would collapse under its own weight. The mathematics behind this also apply to a fairytale giant, twice the size of a normal human. He would weigh eight times more (twice the height, twice the breadth and twice the width), but would be supported by a skeleton only four times as strong (his bones being only twice as wide and twice as broad). To avoid disastrous collapse, more of his body would have to be bone.

It's harder the bigger you get: the size of the biggest land animals is eventually limited by the need to support their massive bodies. Whales, however, are supported by the water around them, so they can evolve to be bigger than even the largest dinosaurs, without having to devote most of their body to mechanical support.

Nevertheless, not all whales are huge. The dwarf sperm whale is about 2.5 metres long, and dolphins and porpoises are really types of small whale. In other words, just because whales *can* evolve enormous bodies, that doesn't mean they will. For that, there must have been advantages in the past to becoming bigger.

We don't know exactly what those advantages were, and they'll differ for different families of whales, but many probably relate to feeding. Large sperm whales not only have more muscle in which to store oxygen, but also use that oxygen at a slower rate, so can dive deeper and longer to hunt for squid. Giant filter feeders, such as blue whales, can grab a lot of tiny sea creatures in a single gulp, as well as going for longer between meals, which is helpful when there are certain areas teeming with food separated by vast expanses of empty ocean. It's possible this happened when climate or ocean currents changed, during the isolation of Antarctica or when the Earth cooled about three million years ago.

WHY DO WE SHIVER WHEN WE ARE COLD?

ASKED BY Ashlyn, age 9

Dr Dawn Harper, *GP and broadcaster, says:*

The human body needs to stay at the same temperature (about thirty-seven degrees Celsius) to keep you alive. If your temperature goes too low or too high it is dangerous for your health.

When you feel cold, tiny sensors in your skin send messages to your brain telling you that you need to warm up, so you put on extra clothes and wrap up warm. Your brain also sends messages to nerves all over your body telling your muscles to tighten and loosen really fast, which is what you recognise as shivering. It does this because when muscles move they generate heat.

As soon as you feel warm again your brain sends more messages telling your muscles to relax and you stop shivering.

HOW DO GEESE CHOOSE THE GOOSE AT THE FRONT OF A FLYING V?

ASKED BY Hamish, age 13

William Fiennes, *author of a book about snow geese, says:*

The thing is, if you look up and watch a V of geese flying overhead, you might notice that it's not always the same goose at the front. Every so often, they change places. This might be because it takes more effort to fly at the front – you're flying straight into the wind, with none of your companions in front of you to provide shelter. So perhaps each goose takes a turn at the front, then drops back to have a rest while another one takes over.

And there's another explanation, too. You know how everyone gets things wrong sometimes? Even your mum and dad, or your cleverest friend? Every now and again, we all get things wrong. It's just the same with geese. The goose at the front of the V is the one leading the way, reading the map inside its head. What if that goose is making a mess of it? Each goose has an idea of the direction they should be flying in. If they take it in turns to go at the front, it won't matter if one of them is terrible at finding the way, because the others will set them on the right course again. By changing places at the front, the geese are more likely to find their way home.

WHO WERE SCARIER, THE VIKINGS OR THE CELTS?

ASKED BY Ripley, age 7

Neil Oliver, *archaeologist, says:*

In a world before police and laws, everywhere was scary. And so was everyone who was better than you at fighting, or who had bigger swords!

Though here's a funny thing – you could say there were no such people as Celts or Vikings. 'Viking' was originally a verb rather than a noun, so it's something you did, rather than something you were. Around 1,000 years ago the people of Denmark, Norway and Sweden liked setting sail in their long-ships in search of adventure. They called this 'going viking' – but they didn't call themselves 'Vikings'.

'Celt' is mostly a word used by teachers to describe the sort of person who lived all over Europe until about 1,500 years ago, by which time the Roman Empire was taking up so much space there was hardly any room for anyone else. In the same way, people in America or Asia might call you 'European', but you probably don't describe yourself that way. Perhaps you say you're 'Scottish' or 'Welsh' or maybe 'Cornish', or any one of loads of names that make more sense to you.

To answer your question, I'd say whichever person was fastest, bravest, strongest and more cunning on the day!

HOW DOES A BABY CHOOSE IF IT'S A BOY OR A GIRL?

ASKED BY Imaad, age 5

Dr Radha Modgil, *GP, medical journalist and presenter, says:*

A round egg is made every month in a mum's body, but that egg can only make a baby if it meets a sperm from the dad.

Sperm look a little bit like tadpoles and can swim fast up into the mum's body from the dad's body. Both eggs and sperm contain a special package of information called chromosomes, which is like a code. It is this package of information that decides if the baby will be a boy or a girl.

A sperm can contain an X chromosome code or a Y code. Eggs always hold an X code. The sperm and egg meet inside the mum's body in the womb. If the first sperm to reach that egg also has an X chromosome, the baby will be a girl (XX). If the first sperm to reach that egg holds a Y chromosome, the baby will be a boy (XY).

So really the baby doesn't have a choice, it is down to random chance!

WHY DO CATS ALWAYS LAND ON THEIR FEET?

ASKED BY CONNOR, AGE 12

Celia Haddon, *author and pet agony aunt, says:*

Cats land on their feet because they can twist their bodies while falling. During a very short fall there is not enough time for them to do this. But if a cat is dropped from, say, a metre, even though it is upside down with its legs facing upwards, it has time to right itself and land on its feet. The fall takes only half a second, but in that time the cat has twisted its whole body around.

This is how it is done. First, the cat bends slightly in the middle, then it tucks in its front legs and sticks out its back legs. This means that its front half twists downwards while the back half is still pointing upwards. Next, the cat straightens out its front legs ready for landing and tucks in its rear legs, so that the back half catches up and all four legs are pointing downwards.

But please don't throw your cat out of the window!

Even though it will probably land on its feet, the
impact of landing might break its legs or its chest.

WHERE DO FINGERNAILS COME FROM?

ASKED BY Shawana, age 10

Professor Alice Roberts, *anatomy expert and broadcaster, says:*

There are several answers to this question. Most mammals have claws, but primates – including us – have flat claws, or fingernails. Before you were born, when you were a tiny developing embryo, your fingernails were formed from the outer layer of cells called 'ectoderm', which also produced your skin, the enamel of your teeth, and your brain and spinal cord.

Your fingernails grow continuously. That's why you need to cut them to keep them short. There's a collection of special cells at the base of the nail, underneath the whitish, half-moon-shaped 'lunula', which continually produces new fingernail cells. If you damage a fingernail or even lose it completely, as long as those special cells are still there, you'll grow another one.

COULD WE LIVE ON ANOTHER PLANET?

ASKED BY Maddie, age 10

Professor Christopher Riley, *science writer and broadcaster, says:*

To answer this question you've got to think hard about all the things you need right now to live here on the surface of the Earth.

In the time it's taken you to read that sentence, you've inhaled just under a litre of air. That's about the same volume as two adult fists. If you were moving, rather than sitting down as you probably are right now, then you'd be inhaling even more air. About twenty-one per cent of this air is oxygen. The rest is almost all nitrogen with some tiny traces of other gases. But it's the oxygen that's most important to keep you alive and healthy.

To stay healthy you'll also have to drink between two and three litres of water today, and eat enough food to give you the energy your body needs. That's probably between two and three kilograms of food, depending on what you like to eat.

Then there are other, less obvious things that are keeping you comfortable right now. You probably like a temperature of around fifteen degrees Celsius, maybe even a bit warmer. You can of course put on a jumper or a coat to keep warm if it's cold. But the point is that there's a narrow range of temperatures that you can survive within, before you'd start to feel unwell.

You are also surrounded by an air pressure of what's called 1 bar (that means a weight of one kilogram of air pressing on each square centimetre of your skin). Without this pressure you'd struggle to breathe, and at very low air pressures the fluids in your skin and eyes would start to boil, which would not be good! You also don't like too much strong sunlight or radiation like X-rays and gamma rays, which come from the Sun and from other stars in the sky. The Earth's atmosphere and its magnetic field protect us from a lot of stuff in space that could harm us.

Humans need such conditions to survive because we have evolved here on the surface of the Earth during a time when these conditions existed. So unless another planet had these same conditions, along with plenty of air, food and water, then we might not be able to live there.

But wait. There's another solution. We could still live on a planet that didn't have these conditions by using our engineering skills. Just as we did by designing and building space suits in the 1960s and '70s which allowed twelve human beings to walk around on the Moon and explore it.

The Moon has none of the things listed above that we need to stay alive, so for the Apollo Moon missions we took them with us. The astronauts carried enough food and water and air and power and shelter inside their spacecraft to survive away from the Earth for up to twelve days. And their space suits provided them with the key things they needed to survive when they were walking around on the surface of the Moon. So humans have already lived on another world for a short time and one day we might do that again!

WHY DO FLOWERS SMELL NICE?

ASKED BY Louie, age 3

Alys Fowler, *gardening writer and broadcaster, says:*

When you smell a beautifully scented flower, all you want to do is smell it again and again. And that's exactly what the flower wants. Except the flower is not at all interested in you. It wants to attract pollinators such as bees, butterflies, beetles and birds.

You may ask: why do flowers need pollinators to visit them? As you know, plants don't have feet. If a plant wants to find a partner so that it can cross-pollinate and make seeds, it needs a bit of help. This is where the pollinator – the insect or bird – comes in. It knows that where there is a wonderful scent, there's a treat. Usually that's sweet-tasting nectar, pollen or other parts of the plant to eat.

The plant lures in the pollinator with a tasty treat and then sticks some of its pollen onto it. When the pollinator visits another flower for a treat, the pollen is transferred from one plant to another. This means cross-pollination happens and new seeds are made.

Not all flowers smell nice. There's a group of plants called 'aroids' that smell of rotting meat or dung. They smell so bad when in flower that you can barely get near them. This is because they are trying to attract dung beetles to come and visit their flowers and pollinate them. What smells horrid to us smells heavenly to that beetle.

HOW DO WE KNOW HOW MANY PEOPLE THERE ARE IN THE WORLD?

ASKED BY James, age 10

Professor Hans Rosling, *doctor and statistician, says:*

Because they have all been counted. At least every ten years each country counts its inhabitants, often by dividing the country into small areas and letting a team of students spend one to two weeks in each area visiting all families and listing all members of each household or family.

That's *how* they count. What they *know* from counting is that the number of people in the world is now around 7 billion. (That's 7,000,000,000.) According to experts at the United Nations Population Division, this number is expected to rise to 9 billion in 2050. That's an increase of 2 billion people over the next thirty-seven years.

But guess what? These experts can tell us that the number of children born each year is not expected to rise in the future. In fact, the number of children alive in the world hasn't risen since 2005. Right now there are around 2 billion children aged fifteen and under, and this should stay roughly the same for the rest of the century.

So where will the 2 billion extra people come from, to reach 9 billion in 2050? Look around you: the people who will cause the increase are already here! The same number of babies may arrive every year, but the world population gets bigger because people who already exist grow up and replace older age groups that don't include so many people – such as my group who were born in the 1940s.

HAS ANYONE CLIMBED EVERY MOUNTAIN?

ASKED BY Sandy, age 11

Patrick Morrow, *mountaineer and photographer, says:*

It would be impossible for one person to climb all the mountains in the world, as there are hundreds of thousands of them. But I've climbed some of the highest. Like you, I was curious about what it would be like to travel the world and climb mountains, so in 1983 I set out to reach and climb the highest peak on all seven continents: Mount Everest, which is the highest in Asia, Mount Aconcagua in South America, Mount McKinley in North America, Kilimanjaro in Africa, and so on.

On my travels, I got to meet and photograph many interesting people who live around those mountains. And of course while I was climbing the peaks, I could see many others that I'd like to visit some day. One of my favourite mountains is Kilimanjaro, because you climb up through all the major climatic zones in the world, from rainforest at the bottom to alpine desert at the top.

Even if you don't climb a mountain, it's exciting and rewarding to make the effort to reach its base, especially if it is situated in a wild, untouched place.

Melting snow and glacier ice in mountains are the source of much of the world's drinking water and it's important for us to try and keep that source as clean as possible. The mountain world can also serve to raise your spirits and its forests provide a breath of fresh air for us and all living things.

WHICH SHAPE HAS THE MOST SIDES?

ASKED BY Ethan, age 8

Marcus du Sautoy, *mathematician, says:*

A circle.

It may seem a strange answer but to a mathematician this is a shape with infinitely many sides.

A triangle has three sides. A square has four sides. A pentagon five. A hexagon six . . . Just as we can keep adding one to numbers, we can keep adding sides to our shapes. If you keep on doing this, drawing the shapes each time, then it becomes harder and harder to see the sides. The more sides a shape has, the more it looks like a circle. So a circle is a shape with infinitely many sides.

Mathematicians used this trick of thinking about the circle as a shape with many sides to first try to work out one of the most important numbers in mathematics: pi.

The number pi is the circumference of a circle divided by its diameter. That is, the distance round the edge of the circle divided by the distance from one side of the circle to the other. Pi is the same number however big or small your circle.

The Greek mathematician Archimedes drew a shape with ninety-six sides around a circle and used the geometry he knew to measure the perimeter of the ninety-six-sided shape. Then he divided that by the diameter of the circle. The answer was 22/7.

This gave the estimate for pi that many engineers use today. But it's not exact. Just an estimate. One of the great discoveries about pi is that it can't actually be written as a fraction. As a decimal number it starts 3.14159 . . . and then the decimal numbers carry on to infinity, never repeating themselves.

WHY DO WE HAVE BOOKS?

ASKED BY Ottilie, age 9

Maria Popova, *writer, says:*

Some people might tell you that books are no longer necessary now that we have the internet. Don't believe them. Books help us know other people, know how the world works, and, in the process, know ourselves more deeply in a way that has nothing to with what you read them on and everything to do with the curiosity, integrity and creative restlessness you bring to them.

Books build bridges to the lives of others, both the characters in them and your countless fellow readers across other lands and other eras, and in doing so elevate you and anchor you more solidly into your own life. They give you a telescope into the minds of others, through which you begin to see with ever greater clarity the starscape of your own mind.

And though the body and form of the book will continue to evolve, its heart and soul never will. Though the telescope might change, the cosmic truths it invites you to peer into remain eternal like the Universe.

In many ways, books are the original internet – each fact, each story, each new bit of information can be a hyperlink to another book, another idea, another gateway into the endlessly whimsical rabbit hole of the written word. Just like the web pages you visit most regularly, your physical bookmarks take you back to those book pages you want to return to again and again, to reabsorb and relive, finding new meaning on each visit – because the landscape of your life is different, new, 'reloaded' by the very act of living.

WHAT IS THE MOST DANGEROUS SEA CREATURE?

ASKED BY Poppy, age 8

Dr Paul Snelgrove, *marine biologist, says:*

You might think of sharks as the deadliest sea creatures but I would not place them high on my list.

To pick out the single most dangerous sea creature is tricky because it depends how you define 'dangerous' and whether we are good at avoiding that creature. For example, many people consider box jellyfish (also known as sea wasps) the most venomous species in the sea but we usually shut down beaches as soon as they are spotted. Stonefish in the tropics can also sometimes kill you if you step on their spines.

Other creatures can be deadly when you eat them. Fugu, or pufferfish, which some people eat raw as sushi, can be lethal if it has not been prepared carefully to remove the highly poisonous liver. But chefs who prepare fugu are highly trained so poisoning is very rare.

Tiny, toxic dinoflagellates, less than a millimetre in size, may be eaten by molluscs such as mussels

and build up in their tissues. If we then eat the con-
taminated mussels they could kill us in extreme
cases. You see, small creatures can be just as deadly, or more so, than big ones!

HOW DEEP DO YOU HAVE TO DIG FOR DINOSAUR BONES?

ASKED BY Sofia, age 10

Dr Paul Barrett, *dinosaur expert, says:*

Usually, scientists digging for dinosaur bones, who are called palaeontologists (pay-lee-on-to-lo-jists), spend their time looking at cliffs and hillsides for fossils that are starting to appear from the rock. After being hidden for millions of years, these buried bones are revealed on the surface by the natural processes of erosion: years of wind, rain, movements of animals through the soil and the growth of plant roots that slowly break the rocks down.

Once bones start to show at the surface, palaeontologists dig around them and under them to remove them. The depth of the hole depends on the size of the bones or skeletons being removed: large animals might need a deep pit to be dug around them of a metre or more, but others that are much smaller only need shallower pits.

It is very rare for a palaeontologist to start digging down to find bones without something showing at the surface first – otherwise they might waste a lot of time and energy digging in an area where there are no fossils to be found.

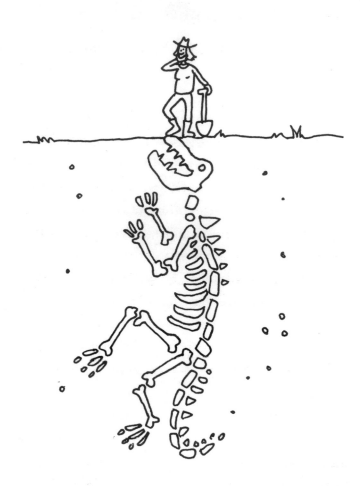

DO BABIES THINK IN WORDS OR THEIR OWN LANGUAGE?

ASKED BY Emerson, age 8

Dr Charles Fernyhough, *psychologist and author, says:*

Babies do some very intelligent things. For example, they seem to have a simple understanding of what objects are and how they behave, and even a basic grasp of numbers. But some psychologists wonder whether babies really 'think' in the way that older children and adults do.

When we think about 'thinking', we tend to see it as talking to yourself in words. When I'm busy with a thought, for example, I'm aware of a voice in my head asking questions and then answering them. But how can you do that before you have any language?

There's no reason to believe that babies use a different language for thinking. Instead, when ordinary language develops it allows little kids to talk to themselves in the way that you or I do. Many psychologists believe that a child's intelligence

157

becomes more powerful when he or she is able to use language in this way. At first, children tend to do this out loud, as you will know if you've ever watched a small child solving a puzzle or playing with their toys. This kind of language is known as 'private speech', and it's thought to have a very important part to play in the development of thinking.

In a sense, then, you could say that babies do clever things and show considerable intelligence in how they make sense of the world, but they don't 'think' until they have language. And it's not some special language that's needed, just ordinary words.

DOES YOUR HAIR GROW WHEN YOU'RE DEAD?

ASKED BY Gavin, age 12

Caitlin Doughty, *mortician and author, says:*

If you're alive (and if you're reading this, I'm going to assume that you are) the hair on your head is growing by a tiny amount every single day. But when you die, all the things your body has been doing on a daily basis will stop. Your heart will stop beating, your blood will stop flowing, and your hair will stop growing.

For thousands of years people believed that a dead person's hair could keep growing because they could actually see it happening! They noticed the very same thing with the dead person's fingernails. They believed both had to be true, because it's hard to argue with things we see with our own eyes.

It turns out, though, that a dead person's hair or fingernails aren't actually growing. The rest of their body is *shrinking*. When you die, your body becomes dehydrated. The plump, moisturised

skin you have in life shrivels up in death, like an
Egyptian mummy. So hair and fingernails may look
longer, but it's actually an illusion caused by the
skin shrinking and pulling back, revealing more of
what was already there.

HOW LONG WOULD IT TAKE A TORTOISE TO RUN ROUND A FOOTBALL PITCH?

ASKED BY Neil, age 11

Matt Parker, *stand-up mathematician*

There are two things we need to know: how fast is the tortoise, and how far is it around the football pitch? I'm sure that, like humans, some tortoises are very sporty and like to run, while others would rather be reading a book. Then there is the matter of why the tortoise is running: is it out for a leisurely stroll just to get some exercise or is it chasing after someone who has annoyed it? There can be a lot of variation in tortoise speed. A slow tortoise walking along will travel 3.5 metres every minute while a fast one can run eight metres in a minute.

Unlike tortoise speeds, you would expect all football pitches to be the same. But they're not. According to the Football Association, a pitch can be anywhere from ninety metres to 120 metres long and between forty-five metres and ninety metres wide. That's a big difference: it means the perimeter (the distance all the way round the pitch) can be anywhere between 270 metres and 420 metres. So an angry, motivated tortoise could get around the smallest possible pitch in only thirty-three minutes and forty-five seconds, while a leisurely tortoise could take up to two hours to get around the biggest pitch and back to its book.

WHAT WILL HOUSES BE LIKE IN THE FUTURE?

ASKED BY Katelin, age 7

Kevin McCloud, *author, broadcaster and designer, says:*

Houses in the future – at least in the near future – will look like the houses we see around us now. There are 26 million of them already in Britain and we're not going to knock them all down. Many of them will be still standing in 2050. But under the skin of our buildings there are big changes happening. We're living through the most exciting time since the industrial revolution because the changes in technology happening all around us are affecting every aspect of our lives.

We're using this technology to update older houses and make them better at saving energy. Meanwhile, the homes that we're beginning to build now are super-insulated. The better ones can keep cool in summer and warm in winter. The homes that my business is building have clever gizmos like solar panels and heat pumps, but this technology will probably be replaced in the next ten years with more efficient versions.

The most interesting area of development lies in computer software. We're already wiring our houses with touch screens that allow you to control the heating and air flow, check how much energy and water you use, keep an eye on your bills, look up local bus times exactly when you need them, connect to a community intranet, book a car from the local car club and plug into your local community. I'm excited by technology that helps us get to know the people who live around us, and helps us to live more easily and cheaply!

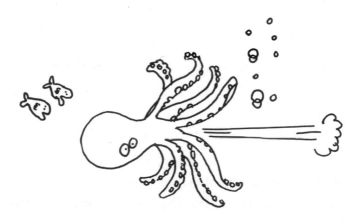

DO OCTOPUSES FART?

ASKED BY Sally, age 6

Professor Joy S. Gaylinn Reidenberg,
comparative anatomist, says:

Yes! All animals fart, including marine animals. I published the first photograph of a whale farting. It looked like a cluster of small bubbles rising from the anus (the same hole where poop comes out, between the belly and the tail).

Octopuses can squirt out ink or pump out water while swimming. These are not farts. When an octopus farts, it can't hide it. We would see bubbles underwater. That's because farts are made of gases. Fart gas is produced by bacteria that live in the intestines. Bacteria are very tiny living things, like germs. However, not all bacteria will make you sick. Some bacteria are good for you because they help you eat.

When an animal eats, it passes the food from its mouth to its stomach and into its intestines. The good bacteria living in the intestines now have an important job to do. They break down the food into smaller pieces that can be used by the animal. When bacteria do this, they make tiny gas bubbles. (You could say they are burping or farting too, but since they don't have a mouth or an anus, it's hard to know for sure.) There are a lot of bacteria making a lot of little burp-farts that combine into a large gas bubble. It is this gas that gets pushed out as a fart.

Breaking down plants produces a lot more gas than breaking down other animal bodies. I've watched manatees fart. They are famous for farting because they only eat underwater plants. Plant-eaters fart more than meat-eaters, but meat-eater farts smell worse! This is true for humans too. So eat more vegetables, and the next time you fart, blame it on the bacteria!

HOW ARE THE NORTHERN LIGHTS MADE?

ASKED BY Cameron, age 10

Dr Heather Couper, *astrophysicist, says:*

It's all down to the Sun! Our local star is a giant ball of hot gas, riddled with magnetic fields. The Sun, being made of gas, spins in a way that's very different from a solid planet like the Earth. Its equator spins faster than its poles, twisting up its magnetic field like a pile of elastic bands.

Pressure builds up until, roughly every eleven years, the Sun breaks out in a rash of sunspots. These are cooler areas where the magnetism holds back the Sun's churning gases. Eventually something has to give and the sunspots erupt, hurling electrically charged particles into space. If Earth is in the firing line, these electric particles head for our polar regions, where our planet's own magnetism is at its strongest. When they hit the atmosphere, these energetic particles light up the sky like gas in a neon tube.

The Northern and Southern Lights can be spectacular – looking like swaying red and green curtains or luminous arcs. They're really spooky! You can take special tours by plane to the Arctic Circle to see the Northern Lights. Although they're best seen from latitudes north of Scotland, I've seen a really powerful display of the Northern Lights from just outside Oxford.

WHY IS METAL SO STRONG?

ASKED BY Oliver, age 7

Professor Mark Miodownik, *engineer and materials scientist, says:*

Metals are made of crystals. Amazing but true. There are billions and billions of tiny metal crystals inside a paperclip, for instance. Most people can't see them because metals are not see-through, but scientists have developed special ways of looking inside metals, and the crystals we find there are every bit as beautiful and fabulous as diamonds.

Crystals such as diamond are hard because all their atoms are neatly arranged in a regular pattern and so all the atoms support each other to resist cracking. Metal crystals are hard for the same reason. But they have another trick up their sleeve that makes metal crystals special. Inside the crystal there are some parts that are not in a regular pattern – these are called defects. These defects can move around inside the crystals, and when they do that, they change the shape of the metal.

This ability means that metal crystals don't tend

to crack or shatter when hit with a hammer, like most types of crystal. Instead, they flow. The metal's crystals flow! Incredible, I know. This is what makes metals so useful. Imagine a car that shattered in a crash, or a steel spoon that snapped in your mouth. If it wasn't for the flow of metal crystals these things would happen all the time. So it's the strength of metals combined with their ability to squish that makes them so impressive.

IF ORANGES ARE CALLED ORANGES, WHY AREN'T BANANAS CALLED YELLOWS?

ASKED BY Edward, age 9

Philip Gooden, *author of books about words, says:*

With some fruit and vegetables the colour came first and was then stuck on like a luggage label: think of redcurrants or blackcurrants or greens. But with oranges it seems to be the other way round, because it was the fruit that gave its name to the colour. Before then if you wanted an expression for 'between red and yellow' you'd have to say just that or something like it.

But bananas don't follow this colour and name pattern. Among other places, Africa was the original source of bananas, and there the word was the name of the plant that produced them, so hundreds of years ago people from Spain and Portugal simply took the word, as they took the fruit, and brought both back to Europe. We've been using the word for a long time now so it doesn't sound as strange as it must have done once. And, to be honest, 'Fancy a banana?' sounds a lot more appetising than 'Would you like a yellow?'

IS SILENCE A SOUND?

ASKED BY Callum, age 9

Quentin Cooper, *science and arts broadcaster and writer, says:*

No. Yes. Depends what you mean.

Sound is a vibration that wobbles its way from the thing making a noise to whoever or whatever hears it. It does that by travelling through something: in our case, usually through air, but it can go through liquids and solids too. If nothing causes such vibrations, or there is nothing for them to travel through (for example in the vacuum of space where there is no air), then there is no noise and the silence we perceive is not a sound, but an absence of all sounds.

There are kinds of silence though – such as the minute's silence before some sports matches – which can have a distinct sound because even if the supporters all keep quiet, together they still make a noise that can be very similar from game to game. And even if you do manage to find somewhere utterly free from all external noises, you are likely

to still hear blood pumping or other very quiet bod-
ily noises. So you could say the sound of silence is
yourself.

WHY CAN'T I KEEP A PENGUIN IN MY BATH?

ASKED BY Jessica, age 8

Zuzana Matyasova, *zookeeper at ZSL London Zoo, says:*

Penguins can look very cute and they are really amazing birds so it's tempting to want one in your house. But there are lots of reasons why you shouldn't keep a penguin in your bath.

Penguins normally live by the sea, where they spend lots of time swimming and the water is very salty. Your bath wouldn't be big enough for a penguin to swim in and the water that comes out of the tap wouldn't be salty – it would take lots and lots of salt to make it just right.

Although penguins love the water, they also like to spend time on land away from the sea. They lay their eggs on land, and if they lived in your bath they would find it very difficult to get out, as the sides are too slippery!

They are really sociable birds and live in big colonies. So your penguin would get very lonely. Also, they are really well suited to living outside – they even have waterproof feathers and special flippers, so it wouldn't like spending all day inside.

Penguins eat lots of fish and this means they often smell like fish too – which wouldn't be very nice in your bathroom! They're really quite messy animals and poo in the water, so you'd have to spend hours and hours cleaning up.

HOW MANY GALAXIES ARE THERE IN THE WHOLE UNIVERSE?

ASKED BY James, age 9

Professor Christopher Riley, *science writer and broadcaster, says:*

During the Christmas holidays of 1995 a group of astronomers decided to try and answer this question by pointing the massively powerful Hubble Space Telescope at a tiny bit of sky near a constellation called the Plough. The patch of sky they were interested in was very small indeed when seen with their bare eyes – about the size of a grain of rice held at arm's length.

Most of the astronomers thought it was a patch of sky that was empty, and no one expected to see very much. But by instructing the Hubble Telescope to look constantly at this tiny piece of sky for ten days they figured that they had a chance of catching even the faintest light which might be coming from anything up there. But no one knew for sure what they would see, so it was a real experiment.

And the picture that resulted from this tiny bit

of sky surprised everyone, for it appeared to be full of hundreds of tiny specks of light. And the closer they looked at each speck the more incredible the picture appeared to be. Almost all of the 3,000 specks of light in the image were in fact entire galaxies, each containing perhaps 200 billion stars!

This famous image is called the Hubble Deep Field and it transformed our view of how many galaxies there are likely to be in the whole Universe. It was so exciting that three years later an identical experiment was done with Hubble to look at the southern sky. Once again the resulting image was packed with galaxies.

Now don't forget that these images are of very tiny bits of sky – and if we multiply them up to the entire sky we find there could be around 350 billion galaxies in the Universe. Maybe more. It's still hard to say exactly how many, as we can only observe a fraction of the Universe. It could even be as many as a trillion!

WHY DO WE HAVE FEELINGS?

ASKED BY Kay, age 9, and Conner, age 10

A. C. Grayling, *philosopher, says:*

Human beings have feelings because we are social animals, and our relationships with others depend on what we feel towards them. Feelings of kindness, love, friendship and concern are very important for bonding us together in our families and communities.

Sometimes, of course, we feel angry or hurt when things go wrong, and this is important too, because it tells us that the relationships causing these feelings need to be changed. We have bad emotions as well as good ones — hate, envy and jealousy are examples of emotions that can be very destructive. But the good feelings of love and pleasure are those that make life worth living, and we can be very glad that we have them.

HOW DO WE STAY ON ROLLER COASTERS WHEN THEY TURN UPSIDE DOWN?

ASKED BY Craig, age 12

Professor Jim Al-Khalili, *scientist and broadcaster, says:*

This is one of those weird situations in science that can be very puzzling when you first think about it, but once explained actually makes complete sense.

Think about it this way: all moving objects, whether footballs, planets or, in this case, roller coasters, will always want to keep going in the same direction they are travelling in. The only reason anything changes its direction of travel from a straight line is if something forces it to. So, for example, the Earth goes round the Sun because the Sun's gravity pulls it round, otherwise our planet would just drift off into deep space. With the roller coaster, it is the rails themselves that force the carriage, and you strapped inside it, to bend round in a loop.

Of course, you have to be travelling fast enough, because when you are upside down there is another force trying to pull you crashing down to the ground: gravity. In fact, because gravity is doing part of the work of trying to pull you round, the rails don't have to press so hard on the wheels. If you go too slowly, the carriage won't have enough forward motion to keep its wheels stuck to the track and gravity will win. That's why the loops on roller coasters always come after a big drop – that's when you're travelling at your fastest.

WHAT IS THE BIGGEST INSECT IN THE WORLD?

ASKED BY Amber, age 7

Dr George McGavin, *entomologist, says:*

The longest is a stick insect called Chan's Megastick from Borneo. The body alone measures 35.7 centimetres and with the legs extended it is 56.7 centimetres long.

But the heaviest insects are probably some of the Goliath beetles from Africa. They can weigh between sixty and 100 grams, making them heavier than many birds. Another beetle, the Titan beetle from South America, although not as heavy as a Goliath beetle, is large – up to seventeen centimetres long – and has super-strong jaws which could give you a very painful nip!

The Birdwing butterflies of South East Asia and Australasia have very large wingspans (up to 280 millimetres) but the largest wing area of any insect is probably that of the Atlas moths of South East Asia – up to 400 square centimetres, which is nearly as big as a square of kitchen towel.

Three hundred million years ago in the Carbon-
iferous Period, when there was more oxygen in
the atmosphere than there is today, many insects
were giants. Large cockroach-like species scuttled
through the humid forests and enormous dragon-
flies whirred through the air on wings nearly one
metre across.

WHEN'S THE BEST TIME OF YEAR TO GO TO ALASKA?

ASKED BY Neil, age 11

Marcel Theroux, *travel writer and author, says:*

Do you like cold weather? I love it. I love snow. I love ice. I love the feeling of cold air in my nostrils. And I love going inside to warm up afterwards.

Most people visit Alaska in summer. It's warmer. The days are longer. It's easier to get around. The weather is more predictable. There are more birds and animals to see. You can spend more time outside. You don't have to take so many warm clothes.

However, I would rather visit Alaska in winter. Yes, you need to wrap up warm. But there are so many things to do. You can stand on a frozen lake and fish through an ice hole. You can ride a snowmobile or a dog sled. You can ski. You can even take all your clothes off and jump into a hot spring. Best of all, you can see the Northern Lights, the swirly, multicoloured natural firework display which is only visible between September and March.

HOW MANY LANGUAGES ARE THERE IN THE WORLD?

ASKED BY Skye, age 9

Professor David Crystal, *language expert, says:*

Somewhere between 6,000 and 7,000. It's not possible to give an exact figure, and it's interesting to know why. Here are three reasons.

We occasionally discover new languages. In some of the mountains, valleys and forests of the world there are small groups of people who may speak a language we don't yet know about. It's really exciting when we find one of these. But it doesn't happen very often.

Sometimes we find groups of people living near each other, and we can't be sure whether they speak the same language or not. We notice that each group uses slightly different words and sounds and sentences. Each group understands some of what the other groups say, but not all of it. So, do we call them different languages? Or do we call them different 'dialects' of the same language? There are lots of cases like this around the world.

But the main reason we can't give an exact figure is because many languages are dying out. Hundreds of languages have very few speakers left – sometimes only one or two – and when they die, their language disappears. This is happening all the time. A language is dying out somewhere in the world every few weeks. So the answer to the question is always going to change.

One thing is certain: the figure is getting smaller and smaller, as the months and years go by. It's probably nearer 6,000 now.

WHY DO WE CRY?

ASKED BY Sebastiano and Afzal, age 9,
Berivan and Bukola, age 10, and Aoife, age 8

Claudia Hammond, *psychologist and radio presenter, says:*

It's normal to cry when you feel upset and until the age of twelve boys cry just as often as girls. But when you think about it, it is a bit strange that salty water spills out from the corners of your eyes just because you feel sad.

One professor noticed people often say that, despite their blotchy faces, a good cry makes them feel better. So he did an experiment where people had to breathe in over a blender full of onions that had just been chopped up. Not surprisingly this made their eyes water. He collected the tears and put them in the freezer. Then he got people to sit in front of a very sad film wearing special goggles which had tiny buckets hanging off the bottom, ready to catch their tears if they cried. The people cried, but the buckets didn't work and in the end he gathered their tears in tiny test tubes instead.

He found that the tears people cried when they were upset contained extra substances, which weren't in the tears caused by the onions. So he thinks maybe we feel better because we get rid of these substances by crying and that this is the purpose of tears.

But not everyone agrees. Many psychologists think that the reason we cry is to let other people know that we need their sympathy or help. So crying, provided we really mean it, brings comfort because people are nice to us.

Crying when we're happy is a bit more of a mystery, but strong emotions have a lot in common, whether happy or sad, so they seem to trigger some of the same processes in the body.

HOW MANY FISH ARE THERE IN THE SEA?

ASKED BY Holly, age 9

Dr Paul Snelgrove, *marine biologist, says:*

This question is harder than it sounds! We don't really have a good estimate of the total number of fish in the sea because they vary so much in size and number, and we have to use different methods to count big and small fish as they move around the oceans. The small ones are especially hard to count because they can hide so easily, and because there is so much ocean – more than ninety-five per cent of the planet that supports life is in the ocean!

Imagine the biggest and smallest fish – a fifteen-metre whale shark next to an infantfish, which, at just under one centimetre, is more than 1,500 times smaller. You'd need an awful lot of those infant-fish to match one whale shark! And finding 1,500 infantfish is much harder than finding one whale shark. We're also talking very big numbers here. One study documented a single school of herrings that contained more than 250 million fish and covered an area the size of Manhattan Island. So we know there are many, many billions of fish in the sea but we don't have a precise number.

We do have a good idea of how many different *types* of fish live in the sea, but even then we can only estimate. Scientists have worked out there are about 16,800 different *known* species of marine fish. But we also discover new species all the time – over 100 marine fish every year!

So how many more until we know them all? Using different approaches, scientists think there are another 5,000 or so more fish species yet to be discovered, many coming from coral reefs and from deep parts of the ocean. Based on current rates of discovery it will take about forty years to find most of those.

WHAT ARE BUTTERFLIES IN MY TUMMY?

ASKED BY Alfie, age 10

Dr Rob Hicks, *GP, medical journalist and presenter, says:*

Well, they're not real butterflies! It's a feeling we get when we feel worried about something like performing in front of people at a school concert, or even when we are excited but a bit nervous about something like going to a party.

When we feel worried, nervous or frightened, our body makes a chemical called adrenaline that puts us into what is called 'fight or flight mode', or on 'red alert'. It means we're ready for action, either to stay and fight what's making us feel like this, or to run away from it. For example, imagine you're faced with a bully at school. You can stay and confront ('fight') them, or turn and walk away ('flight') from them.

Adrenaline automatically prepares our bodies to think and move quickly by making the heart beat faster to pump more blood to the muscles, and making us breathe in air faster to get more oxygen. The stomach becomes smaller so it needs less blood to work – which means there's more blood for other parts of the body such as the muscles and brain that need plenty of blood to help us react fast. As this happens we feel butterflies in the tummy.

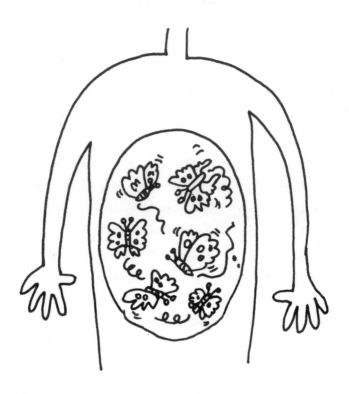

DOES ICE SMELL?

ASKED BY Megan, age 10

Dr Gabrielle Walker, *writer and broadcaster on climate change, says:*

Ice is just frozen water, so it would only smell if you mixed it up with something smelly. But sometimes you CAN smell ice the way you might sniff a rose.

When ice forms thick sheets in Greenland and at the South Pole, it doesn't freeze directly from water but instead starts off as snow. The snow is full of air, which is why it's so fluffy. When snow falls on top of more snow, the weight starts to squeeze the fluffy snowflakes until they become glued together into ice, trapping the air.

In places like the South Pole, it's so cold that ice never melts but just keeps getting thicker and thicker. Eventually scientists can stand on top of this 'ice mountain' and drill down into the ice, going backwards in time as they drill into deeper and deeper layers. I've been there when they do it and it's amazing to see. They have managed to pull out ice that is 800,000 years old – and still contains bubbles of ancient air.

When I was there, they put some of this old ice in a drink to celebrate and I could hear those ancient bubbles going 'pop, crackle, pop' as the ice melted. And then I sniffed the air coming out of my glass. That air was buried in ice before humans existed, so I knew I was the first person ever to smell it. To be honest, it smelt just like normal air, but it was still very exciting.

HOW CAN WE STOP AN ASTEROID HITTING EARTH?

ASKED BY Paul, age 14

Marcus Chown, *author of books about space and the Universe, says:*

Asteroids are the builders' rubble left over from the birth of the solar system 4.55 billion years ago. Most of these chunks of rock circle the Sun between the orbits of Mars and Jupiter. But sometimes two asteroids bump into each, and one or both is kicked out of the 'asteroid belt'. These may end up on a collision course with the Earth. One such asteroid – about the size of a small city – is believed to have wiped out the dinosaurs 65 million years ago.

If we discover an asteroid that will hit us very soon, there will be nothing we can do to stop it. But if there are a few years before it is due to hit, we may be able to deflect it. It will be difficult. A spacecraft will have to fly to the asteroid and land on it. Blowing up the asteroid with a big bomb will not work because it will simply turn one big asteroid into dozens of smaller asteroids – all still heading for the Earth!

The best way to deflect the asteroid is probably for the astronauts to grind up some of its rock and fire it at high speed into space. The asteroid will 'recoil' in the opposite direction from the ground-up rock, just like a gun that jumps backwards when it fires a bullet. If the astronauts do this continuously, week after week, month after month, gradually the asteroid will be deflected so that it will miss the Earth.

WHY DO CATS 'MIAOW', COWS 'MOO' AND SHEEP 'BAA'?

ASKED BY Megan, age 10

Professor David Bellos, *translator, says:*

That's a really big question. There's no simple answer to it. The sad fact is that cows speak cow, sheep speak sheep, cats speak cat – and we don't.

'Miaow' is the way that we write down the sound that a cat makes. We pronounce the letters of the word according to the rules of English, not the rules of cat, whatever they are. Cats don't say anything different wherever they are in the world. A Persian cat in a Berlin apartment and a tabby in a Paris restaurant make much the same sound. Cat noise doesn't change, and is made only by cats.

However, when a speaker of Japanese wants to write down the sound her cat makes, she traces the characters ニ ヤ マ. Put into English letters, they would sound like 'nyaa'. We can assume that cats in Japan make the same noise as they do in England. But what Japanese speakers hear is possibly something else.

Likewise, ducks in France say 'coincoin', not quack quack, and in Greece they say πα πα πα (pronounced 'pa pa pa'). Sheep in Japan say ナエ (pronounced 'may', with a slightly longer sound than the name of the month). In Russia, cats make the noise мур-мур, that's to say 'mur-mur', when they are happy; in Albania barking dogs say 'ham ham'.

The ways animal sounds are written down in various languages are sometimes so different that it makes you wonder just what it is we truly hear. Do we hear 'miaow' because that's the sound a cat makes, or do we hear it that way because we've been taught to write it down with those letters?

But perhaps things aren't really so complicated. Lots of languages have words for animal noises that are very similar to each other. For example, dogs go 'wa wa' or 'waff waff' in French, 'woof' in English, 'hav hav' in Modern Hebrew, 'vau vau' in Hungarian, 'vov vov' in Swedish, 'woef' in Dutch and 'wuff wuff' in German. Even in Ancient Egyptian, written in hieroglyphs that were unbelievably hard to decipher, the lion's roar, written ☜, seems to have been sounded out as 'row'. For cat noise they wrote 𓈎𓇋𓂝𓏏 which sounded maybe something like 'miu'.

As to why cats say 'miaow' and cows say 'moo' (except in Thailand, where a *moo* is a pig) . . . that's to say, what makes a cat produce the sound we try to picture through the letters m, i, a o, and w? Well, that's a question you should send to someone who knows exactly what's inside animals' throats and mouths. I mean, someone else.

WHAT MAKES FOOD ROT?

ASKED BY Millie, age 10

Dr George McGavin, *entomologist, says:*

Bacteria make food rot. You can't see them but life on Earth would be impossible without them and together they outweigh all other animals and plants on the planet. A teaspoonful of soil, for instance, may contain 40 billion bacteria. Each one is a single-celled organism. They are found absolutely everywhere: on land, in oceans and rivers and in the air. You have many species of bacteria on your skin and inside your body. In fact, you contain nine times more bacterial cells than human cells.

Bacteria are very important to the way ecosystems work and are essential in the recycling of dead organisms, but some species can cause deadly infections. Certain bacteria are called 'food spoilage bacteria' and these are the ones that cause food to rot. If fresh or cooked food is left out it can quickly start to decay. If it is warm, bacteria can multiply very rapidly making food rot even faster.

Bacteria are not the only organisms that make

food decay. There are spores of another sort of organism drifting around in the air – the fungi. Fungal spores can settle on food and start to grow, making the food mouldy. But moulds can be useful too. Penicillin, the antibiotic medicine, was made from a common mould.

WHY DON'T HUMANS HAVE TAILS?

ASKED BY Ben, age 8

Dr Louise Leakey, *palaeontologist, says:*

None of the great apes have tails and we are one of the seven species of great ape that are alive today on planet Earth. It is important to realise that six of the great ape species are severely threatened and endangered by the extraordinary numbers and impact of the seventh, ourselves, *Homo sapiens*!

Now back to the question of why we humans don't have tails. Well, the main function of a primate's tail is for balance, which is particularly helpful when swinging through tree branches. Great apes are large and mostly live on the ground. Through our evolutionary journey we have lost the need for our long tails.

But do you know that you still have the remnants of your tail? You have a little tailbone that is called the coccyx, and if you fall hard and land on it you can, in fact, break this bone. Sitting on a cushion with a hole in it is the only way you can comfortably sit on a chair while it repairs itself.

Wouldn't it look very funny if people still had tails? What would you do with your tail if you had one?

WHY IS A RAINBOW CURVED?

ASKED BY Holly, age 6

Johnny Ball, *maths and science enthuser, says:*

When you see a rainbow, the Sun is always behind you and your head is in a line with the Sun and where the centre of the rainbow's curve would be. You are the only person in the world who can see that rainbow – even someone standing right next to you will see a rainbow in a slightly different place in the sky.

When rainbows form, there is always water vapour in the air and the Sun's rays bounce off the water drops and back into your eye. The colours are caused by the angles at which the Sun's rays bounce. Every bit of red is produced by rays bouncing at one particular angle. Every bit of blue is caused by a slightly sharper angle of bounce. For this to work, the rainbow has to be in a bow shape with the red at the top.

Sometimes you can see a second rainbow, fainter but outside the first one. This time the colours are reversed and the red is at the bottom.

Quite often when flying in an aircraft, you might see a rainbow on the clouds below you. This time you will also see the shadow of the aircraft right in the centre of the rainbow and if you are lucky, the rainbow will form a complete circle. The dead centre of that rainbow circle is the shadow of the aircraft window your eyes are looking through.

WHAT'S THE WORST FOOTBALL TEAM IN THE WORLD?

ASKED BY Ariana, age 9

Paul Watson, *journalist and author of a football book, says:*

Have you ever heard of a tiny island called Pohnpei in the Pacific Ocean, on the other side of the world? Probably not. Until recently their football team had never won a game. In fact they had lost every game they had ever played, including a 16–1 loss to a nearby island called Guam.

How do I know about Pohnpei? Let me tell you a story. I always loved playing football and dreamed that one day I would play for England, or at least my favourite team, Bristol City.

My problem was that I wasn't very good at football. Some of my friends were signed by professional teams but I was never chosen. Instead of playing football for my job I decided to write about it as a sports journalist, but I still wished I could play for England.

When I was twenty-five I was living with a friend called Matt, who was also mad about football, and we came up with a plan. We knew we weren't good enough to play for England because they are a very good team, but we decided to find the worst football country in the world and try to play for them instead!

So Matt and I moved to Pohnpei. It's a beautiful island and the people are very friendly, but it's one of the wettest places in the world so it rained hard every day. They had one football pitch and it was always flooded, with lots of toads hopping across it! Never mind a crowd to support them – there weren't even any players when we first arrived.

The people loved football though and we created a good team. We trained hard and went to Guam to try and win Pohnpei's first game in a competition there. Most of the players had never been on a plane before and were very excited.

We lost our first two games but in our last match we won 7–1! It was the first time Pohnpei had won and everybody celebrated. Pohnpei might not be the best football team in the world but they enjoy playing and they keep trying and that's what really counts.

WHY DON'T WE HAVE MEMORIES OF WHEN WE WERE BABIES OR TODDLERS?

ASKED BY Maia, age 11

Dr Tali Sharot, *neuroscientist, says:*

We use our brain for memory. In the first few years of our lives, our brain grows and changes a lot, just like the rest of our body. Scientists think that because the parts of our brain that are important for memory have not fully developed when we are babies, we are unable to store memories in the same way that we do when we are older.

Also, when we are very young we do not know how to speak. This makes it difficult to keep events in your mind and remember them later, because we use language to remember what happened in the past.

WHY ARE BUMBLEBEES DISAPPEARING?

ASKED BY Kush, age 12

Tony Juniper, *environmental campaigner and writer, says:*

Bumblebees are those furry, stripy creatures that we see in early spring, buzzing from flower to flower in search of sweet nectar and pollen. Their thick fur keeps them warm in the cold, and that is why they are often the first insects we see out and about as the winter comes to an end. These little creatures are very important in helping plants to make fruit and seed through moving pollen between flowers. Without that help, lots of plants can't reproduce themselves.

There are twenty-six different kinds of bumble-bee known in the UK. Two are already extinct here while several others are fast disappearing. There are several reasons why these bees are becoming scarcer. The main one seems to be the loss of the places they live. Bumblebees like rough grassy places with lots of wild flowers. Many gardens are now covered with gravel and paving, and wilder areas replaced with neat flowerbeds where there are no wild flowers. In the countryside, changes to farming have reduced the places these creatures like. They are also affected by some of the chemicals used to kill pest insects that attack crops.

If you have a garden you can help bumblebees by setting aside areas where wild flowers grow. School grounds and other places can help in the same way. Putting wild areas around farms can bring the bees back. Avoiding chemicals in the garden and around the places we grow food will help too.

HOW CAN I BE A PRINCESS?

ASKED BY Ruby, age 3

Dr Helen Castor, *historian, says:*

There are two ways to become a princess, but no one gets a choice about the first one: if your mum happens to be a queen or your dad is a king, you'll become a princess when you're born.

(In Britain, you're also a princess if you're a grand-daughter of the queen or king – but ONLY if they're your dad's parents, not your mum's. The rules don't always treat women in the same way as men.)

The second way to become a princess is to marry a prince. So in Britain the available options at the moment, if this is your plan, are to marry Prince Andrew or Prince Harry. One thing to watch out for, though, is that this way you don't get to be a princess with your own name. If I married Prince Harry, I wouldn't be Princess Helen, I'd be Princess Harry – a bit like marrying Mr Smith and becoming Mrs Smith.

The other thing to remember is that rules about royal titles keep changing. For most of the Middle Ages, the children of English kings and queens were called 'Lord' and 'Lady', not 'Prince' and 'Princess'. In some ways it's all made up as the royal family goes along – and nowadays being a princess isn't really a job description, so if it's the palace or the tiara that's particularly appealing, you could think about becoming an architect or a jeweller and making your own!

HOW DO TASTE BUDS TASTE?

ASKED BY Kieran, age 9, and Mathanojh, age 8

Dr Mark Porter, *GP and medical journalist, says:*

We all have around 10,000 tiny taste buds in our mouths. You can't really see them because they are so small. And they are not just on the surface of your tongue – there are taste buds on your lips, the inside of your cheeks, the roof of your mouth and the back of your throat too.

The simplest way to think of taste is to compare it to touch. While special nerves in your fingers can tell you whether something is furry or smooth or hot or cold, taste buds tell you whether it is sweet or salty.

In fact there are five basic tastes that your taste buds can pick up: sweet (like cake), sour (like lemon), bitter (like coffee – yuck), salty (like crisps) and umami (like soy sauce or Parmesan cheese).

But it is not just your taste buds that work out how a particular food or drink tastes – smell is important too. And in order to get the real flavour of a curry, a bowl of chips or some tomato soup, your brain combines all the different tastes and smells it receives from the nerves supplying your mouth and nose.

And if you can't smell properly – like when your nose is blocked because of a cold – food and drink doesn't taste as strong. Which is why children often hold their noses when they are eating or drinking something they don't like. Try it and see!

WHY DO MAGNETS ONLY STICK TO METAL?

ASKED BY Rual, age 8, and Leia, age 12

Professor Jim Al-Khalili, *scientist and broadcaster, says:*

You'd think this would be an easy one to explain, but it's not. The short answer is that it's all down to atoms – but that doesn't really tell you much, does it? So let me be a bit clearer.

Everything is made of atoms, and all atoms are themselves made of the same ingredients: a tiny nucleus surrounded by even tinier electrons buzzing around it. And it is these electrons that can give certain kinds of atoms their magnetic properties. When some materials are brought close to a magnet their atoms get stretched out of shape and this turns them into mini magnets themselves. We can zoom in even more and say that it is because each individual electron is basically a spinning electric charge and so is itself a miniature magnet.

Think of all the atoms in a lump of metal as tiny compasses with their needles all pointing in different directions. Bring a magnet close to them and their needles will start to behave in a co-ordinated way and point in one particular direction. The metal has become 'magnetised', and so it will react with the original magnet by sticking to it.

So the big question is this: why don't all atoms behave like this? What is it about the atoms in wood, say, or plastic, that makes them ignore magnets? Here is the tricky bit: the way atoms behave depends on exactly how many electrons they have and how these move around the nucleus. And it isn't simply a case of more electrons making an atom a stronger mini magnet.

Different electrons have their own special ways of organising themselves and moving around a nucleus. It just so happens that the atoms of certain metals have electrons that are easily influenced by magnets.

WHY ARE CHILLIES SO SPICY?

ASKED BY Ruthie, age 7

Madhur Jaffrey, *cookery author, says:*

It is the nature of some vegetables and fruit to be sweet, some to be sour, some to be bitter and some to be nutty. Nature just made them that way. Chilli peppers are, by nature, spicy. They make a chemical called capsaicin, which leaves a burning feeling in our mouths. We think pepper plants do this to stop some animals eating their fruit. Some varieties are a little spicy and others are so hot they could almost blow you away. I like those that are just in the middle – just mildly spicy.

IF THE ICE CAPS ARE MELTING, DOES THAT AFFECT SEA LIFE?

ASKED BY Emily, age 11

Dr Gabrielle Walker, *writer and broadcaster on climate change, says:*

Yes! Lots of creatures make their living using the ice caps and are suffering because of the melting ice.

In the Arctic (up in the north), polar bears need sea ice to hunt from. So when the ice melts that is very bad for the bears, although it might be good for the poor animals they are trying to catch.

In Antarctica (down in the south) there are emperor penguins that are nearly as tall as you! They are dignified and stately and have every right to be proud of themselves because the males spend the entire winter bravely standing on the sea ice, not eating, not moving much, just keeping their eggs warm on their feet and waiting for the spring. The melting ice will make life even harder for these lovely creatures, which is a shame.

But the saddest story of all, I think, is about

tiny little shrimp-like creatures called krill whose babies live under the protection of the ice in great krill nurseries. As the ice melts, the nurseries are disappearing and so are the krill.

That matters because lots of big beautiful sea creatures, such as seals, whales and penguins, need to eat the krill to survive. Instead of the krill, the new conditions favour blobby jellyfish called salps. And although you might like eating jelly, penguins and seals don't!

WHY DON'T SNAKES CHEW THEIR FOOD?

ASKED BY Connor, age 5

Steve Leonard, *vet and wildlife TV presenter, says:*

We chew our food to help break it down into a mush that our guts can then work on. This is because we evolved to eat lots of plant matter, which locks away its nutrients inside fibrous material that needs pulverising between our molar teeth.

Most carnivores do little chewing because the foods they eat (meat, insects, eggs, snails) are very easily digested. Birds of prey and crocodiles rip their prey into small enough chunks to swallow without actually chewing, but snakes have gone one step further. Without the ability to tear their food apart (they have no legs to grab hold of the food like the birds, nor a large heavy body to twist parts off like the crocodile), they have evolved a very flexible lower jaw that allows them to swallow massive meals whole. It would be like you swallowing an entire turkey. This also means they can quickly devour their prey and slink off and hide from competitors or other predators.

In order to cope with these huge meals they have evolved powerful stomach acids that can digest almost all of their prey (though not the teeth, claws, hair or feathers – these come out in the snake's poo). They digest over a long time – months for a large python. The biggest meal I ever saw a snake eat was when a 6.2-metre reticulated python ate a whole wild boar bigger than me. Gulp!

WHY WAS TV INVENTED?

ASKED BY Robyn, age 10

Iain Logie Baird, *Associate Curator at the National Media Museum, says:*

One man's inspiration brought the first television pictures to the world on 26 January 1926. That man was my grandfather, John Logie Baird.

Why did he invent television? He needed to raise some money after ill health forced him to close his soap business in 1923 and move to Hastings, a small town on the south coast of England. Because he wasn't well, he knew that he needed to invent something that was really successful in order to earn his living. He tried pneumatic-soled shoes and a glass razor blade that would never tarnish, but these ideas proved fruitless.

He walked along the nearby cliffs and thought back to his training as an electrical engineer a few years earlier. He realised that technology had improved since his training, and that television was now possible.

Television was a combination of a few older ideas such as the stage play, the telescope, the radio and the cinema. It was a complicated technology. By showing many pictures each second – faster than our eyes and brains can perceive – television creates an illusion of reality. The first televisions used an orange lamp for light and a spinning wheel, which was put in front of the lamp. The outer edge of the wheel had holes, arranged to trace out a picture line by line as the light varied. The pictures, viewed from the other side of the wheel, were small and not very detailed.

Although a handful of engineers, scientists and big companies were working on developing television at the same time, Baird was ahead of them in coming up with the first practical solution to show real images. However, the big companies had more money and people, and were soon able to develop superior systems.

Nonetheless, Baird would stay on the cutting edge of television technology for the rest of his life, developing the first colour television, 3-D television and high-definition colour television.

Televisions today have light coming from behind their large, flat screens, or sometimes from millions of individual cells containing a gas which lights up when electrified. Now the pictures are traced out by a computer chip inside the television.

WHY CAN'T WE BREATHE UNDERWATER? FISH CAN!

ASKED BY Joe, Jane and Zak, age 7, and Abbas, Amal and Rayyan, age 10

Alok Jha, *science journalist, says:*

Our lungs are excellent at taking oxygen out of the air we breathe. Fish also need oxygen to live but, of course, they can't breathe air. So they get their oxygen from the water around them, using a body part called gills.

Water is very good at dissolving oxygen (just like it is good at dissolving salt or sugar if you stir it into a drink). As a fish swims around, water moves through its gills, which are specially adapted to take out the oxygen that is dissolved there.

Our lungs, unfortunately, would never work underwater because they are not strong enough to move water, which is much heavier than air, in and out. As well as that, there is much less oxygen dissolved in water than there is freely floating in the air. So even if we could somehow breathe in water and take out the oxygen like fish do, we would still not be able to get enough oxygen into our bodies with every breath we took. And without enough oxygen, our bodies would stop working properly.

Good job, then, that we live on land, where there is plenty of air around for our lungs to do their work.

WHAT DO ASTRONAUTS EAT?

ASKED BY Charlie, age 9

Dr Kevin Fong, *expert in space medicine, says:*

Inside a spacecraft there isn't much room, there's very little spare power and everything is weightless. All this makes cooking pretty tricky. Imagine trying to cook on an ordinary gas cooker in space. First of all your pots and pans and everything inside them would want to float around. But worse still, the weightlessness would make fire dance around as though it were alive, which would be unpredictable and dangerous.

You can't use an electric cooker either, because it would chew up too much power and it still wouldn't get round the flying saucepan problem! You might think a microwave oven would work but those are very heavy and also eat up too much electricity.

So food has to be prepared and cooked in a very different way. A lot of the food astronauts eat has almost all its water removed before it is launched into space. This is called dehydration and it does two things. First, it makes the food lighter – which means the rocket can carry more – and second, it helps prevent food going off (fridges are also too heavy and too power-hungry). These dried foods are sealed in bags. To warm the food up the astronauts inject hot water into the bags, kind of like pouring hot water on instant noodles. And to eat it they suck it through a straw.

They can eat other foods with a fork or spoon out of a shallow tray. You might think that would be pretty messy, but if it's moist enough – spaghetti hoops, for example – then the water in the food makes it stick together and to the tray.

A typical astronaut meal might have some beef or chicken that's been cooked on Earth and then specially prepared to keep it fresh without having to store it in a fridge. This might be served with some dehydrated vegetables in bags – perhaps broccoli and carrots, to which they'll add hot water. For dessert you might have some dried peaches or a granola bar. (By the way, astronauts avoid fizzy drinks and baked beans in space. Foods that make you burp and fart are not popular with anyone up there!)

The menu is much better than it used to be in the early days of space flight but when it comes to food, nothing beats being back on Earth.

Occasionally the crew aboard the space station get a treat, when they are resupplied with cargo from Earth. Astronauts really look forward to these deliveries because they usually include fresh fruit and vegetables – apples, bananas, celery and carrots – rare luxuries when you're floating in space for months with no fridge and no supermarket.

SHOULD WE ALWAYS BE NICE TO MEAN PEOPLE?

ASKED BY Esther, age 8

Alexander Armstrong, *comedian, actor and TV presenter, says:*

The answer to this one is both simple *and* difficult. Simple because broadly speaking we should always be nice to mean people. The world is a better place if there are more nice people in it than mean people, and so we must try not to become meanies ourselves just because someone else has been mean to us. But that's difficult because it sometimes feels impossible to be nice to someone who has acted in a horrible way. So while it's important that mean people should never get their own way through being unpleasant, we have to remember that people are often nasty because they feel uncomfortable or because they are uncertain of themselves and by being nice to them we can maybe make them feel better, and that way turn them into nicer people.

QUIZZES

Who's the smartest goldfish in your bowl? Take it in turns to quiz your friends and family!

All these quiz questions have also been thought up by children. Can you figure out which of the answers is right?

QUIZ ONE

1. Do all animals have brains? (Victoria, 10)

a. Yes, of course they do.
b. No, some animals get along with no brain.
c. No, only humans have brains.

ANSWER

b. No, some animals get along with no brain.
Echinoderms – a group that includes starfish, sea
urchins and sea cucumbers – have a network of
nerves but no central brain. Tunicates, like the
sea squirt, have a primitive brain called a cerebral
ganglion which controls their swimming. But when
they grow up they attach themselves to a rock and
no longer need this brain, so it disappears. Even
more simple is a group of flat worms called acoelo-
morphs. They have no brain, no gut, no circulatory
system, no respiratory system and no bottom!

2. What are freckles? (Louie, 3)

a. Small brown spots where the skin has produced
extra colour.

b. Signs that the fairies have been kissing you in the night.

c. Scars left after diseases such as chicken pox or measles.

ANSWER

a. Small brown spots where the skin has produced extra colour. Freckles only form on skin that has been exposed to the sun. They occur when the colour-making skin cells (called melanocytes) make lots of the substance melatonin, which turns those skin cells brown. You do not usually get freckles on your skin until after you are five years old, and they often fade when you are grown up.

3. Can penguins fly? (James, 7)

a. Yes, that's what their wings are for.

b. No, they prefer to swim.

c. Yes, but only when they are adult.

ANSWER

b. No, they prefer to swim. Penguins can't fly in the air, and they can only waddle on land. But in the water they use their wings like flippers and can swim extremely fast. In a way, you could say that they actually fly through the water. The fastest swimming penguin is the gentoo penguin, which can swim up to thirty-six kilometres per hour. Almost as fast as Usain Bolt runs the 100 metres!

4. Who invented football? (Israar, 9)

a. The Egyptians.
b. No one really knows.
c. The ancient Chinese.

ANSWER

b. No one really knows. But the game as we know it originated in 1863. The modern game of association football (known as soccer) was created in 1863 when it split from rugby football and the Football Association was formed in England. At the start you could still play with any size of ball as long as both teams agreed – it wasn't until 1872 that teams were expected to play with a ball of standard size and weight.

For many centuries before this, people (including ancient Chinese soldiers, ancient Greeks and Romans) had been kicking a ball around for various reasons, in various games. It is almost impossible to say for certain if any of these games are directly related to the football played today.

5. Is a tomato a fruit or a vegetable?
(Tristan, 8)

a. A fruit.

b. A vegetable.

c. Neither – tomatoes are swollen red leaves.

ANSWER

a. A fruit. Scientifically speaking, tomatoes are fruit because they develop from the flower of the plant, whereas a vegetable is an edible part of the plant itself (stem, root, leaves, etc.). In the kitchen, however, it is usual to speak of a tomato as a vegetable because it is used in savoury cooking, while fruits are used in sweet dishes. The tomato plant originated in the Americas and although people grew them in Europe in the sixteenth century, they only did so because they liked the look of the plants – they thought the fruit were poisonous.

6. Who invented Christmas crackers?
(Anne, 10)

a. A Chinese gun maker.

b. A French magician.

c. A British sweet maker.

c. A British sweet maker. Crackers were invented by a confectioner called Tom Smith. In 1840 Tom took his family on a trip to Paris, then the sweet capital of the world, where he discovered the bonbon, a sugared almond wrapped in a twist of colourful waxed paper. Back in England Tom decided to improve on the bonbon by adding extra things to the wrapper: first a motto and then a small gift. According to Tom he got the idea for the 'snap' one autumn sitting by the fire when a log crackled. It took him two years to develop the cracker snap, which he launched in 1860 with the 'Bangs of Expectation' range. By 1900 Tom's factory was making 13 million crackers a year.

7. Can crocodiles climb stairs?

a. No, they can't lift their legs high enough
b. No, they are afraid of heights.
c. Yes.

ANSWER

c. Yes. Crocodiles do not come across stairs very often, but they have been known to climb them. They have several ways of moving on land, one of which is called the 'high walk', when the crocodile straightens its legs out and lifts its body clear of the ground. Walking in this way it can step over obstacles and climb over things. A more common way of moving on land is the 'belly crawl', when the crocodile lets its body slide along the ground while it crawls along. Amazingly, some species of crocodiles can even gallop or jump.

8. Were there any other names J. K. Rowling considered for the character Harry Potter? (Millie, 10)

a. No, it's her favourite boy's name.
b. Yes, lots. She put them all in a hat and pulled Harry out.
c. She didn't choose it, her publisher ran a competition to pick a name.

ANSWER
a. No, it's her favourite boy's name. In an interview, J. K. Rowling revealed that Harry had always been her favourite boy's name, so she used it. However, if she had had a son instead of a daughter she might have had to choose a different name for her hero because she would have named her

son Harry *before* she wrote the books. The surname Potter was from a family who used to live near her when she was a child.

QUIZ TWO

1. Why is blue cheese mouldy? (Joshua, 8)

a. Because it hasn't been stored properly.

b. A special mould is added to the cheese to give it a distinctive flavour.

c. It's not mould, it's a colouring added to make the cheese look nice.

ANSWER

b. A special mould is added to the cheese to give it a distinctive flavour. The mould, called *Penicillium rocqueforti*, is added to the milk or curd when blue cheese is being made. Long thin holes are made with wire in the cheese to allow the mould to grow and spread, adding to the flavour. The mould in blue cheese is not harmful. Indeed, other species of the *Penicillium* mould are used to make the antibiotic medicine penicillin.

2. Who invented aeroplanes? (Amarah, 8)

a. Eilmer, the flying monk of Malmesbury.

b. Orville and Wilbur Wright.

c. Leonardo da Vinci.

ANSWER

b. Orville and Wilbur Wright. Lots of people have made flying machines over the centuries, but the first aeroplane that had an engine and could carry a person was made by the Wright brothers and flown by Orville Wright near the town of Kitty Hawk in North Carolina, in the USA, in 1903. They owned a bicycle shop and had tested a model in their wind tunnel before they built their plane, which was driven by a propeller and a home-made motor. In the fifteenth century, Leonardo da Vinci designed flying devices, but there is no evidence that he ever tried to build one (and they certainly didn't have engines). Eilmer, a monk living in Malmesbury in England in the eleventh century, made himself a pair of wings and jumped off the church tower. Whoops! He fell rather than flew, and broke both his legs. He wanted to have another go but his abbot wouldn't let him.

3. Which country has the most people?
(Jessica, 6)

a. China.

b. The USA.

c. India.

ANSWER

a. China. The country with the largest population is China, with 1,354,040,000 inhabitants. India has the second largest population. Both China and India are in the continent of Asia, where about three fifths of the people in the world live, even though Asia takes up only about one third of the world's area.

4. Why do bees buzz? (Ella, 5)

a. They don't like humming.

b. To attract a mate.

c. It's the noise their wings make when they fly.

ANSWER

c. It's the noise their wings make when they fly. When bees fly their wings make the air vibrate and this sounds like buzzing. Some bees (particularly bumblebees) can make their bodies vibrate as well and this helps shake pollen from flowers. Some of this pollen is taken back to the hive to feed the bee larvae, but some gets brushed off at the next flower and helps pollinate it. This is called buzz pollination.

5. Does the Moon have weather?
(Djoumana, 10)

a. Yes.

b. No.

c. Yes, but only on the side lit up by the Sun.

ANSWER

b. No. The Moon has no weather because it has almost no atmosphere – less than one hundred trillionth of Earth's. With no snow, rain or wind this means that there is nothing to erase the footprints left by astronauts who have walked on the Moon. However, the temperature on the surface changes dramatically, from as high as 127 degrees Celsius down to as low as minus 173. This is, again, because there is virtually no atmosphere to protect the Moon: the atmosphere around Earth is like a big blanket that stops us from experiencing such extremely high or low temperatures.

6. Why does the Queen get two birthdays? (William, 10)

a. Because she really like parties.

b. In case her family forgets one of them.

c. So that the celebrations take place on a day when the weather is likely to be nice.

ANSWER

c. So that the celebrations take place on a day when the weather is likely to be nice.
The Queen's actual birthday is on 21 April but her official birthday in the UK is on the first, second or third Saturday in June, the exact date being fixed by the government. This means that whatever time of year the king or queen's birthday actually is, the official birthday parade, called the Trooping of the Colour, can take place on a summer's day.

7. Why is Boxing Day called Boxing Day? (Tristan, 8)

a. Because it was the day when fights traditionally broke out in families.

b. Because it was the day when Christmas boxes were given out to staff.

c. Because children used to hide in the boxes their presents had arrived in on this day.

b. Because it was the day when Christmas boxes were given out to staff. The day after Christmas was traditionally when people would give gifts known as Christmas boxes to their staff and tradespeople. It is said that they had to wait until the day after Christmas because servants would have to work on Christmas Day itself. In the UK the Boxing Day holiday is the first weekday after Christmas Day.

8. Why do we have belly buttons?
(Ethan, 5)

a. To store the salt in when you eat chips in bed.
b. To remind you where your tummy is.
c. It's where the umbilical cord was attached when you were a baby in the womb.

c. It's where the umbilical cord was attached when you were a baby in the womb. When a baby is growing in its mother's womb, it is attached to the mother by what is called the umbilical cord. The blood vessels in this cord provide the baby with everything it needs as it can't breathe, eat or drink for itself. When the baby is born it can breathe and eat on its own, so the umbilical cord is removed. A small stump of cord is usually left for a few days, but that withers and falls off (the baby doesn't feel anything) and the mark it leaves on the baby's tummy is the belly button or navel.

QUIZ THREE

1. What is the most popular food in the world? (Skye, 9)

a. Pizza.
b. Rice.
c. Chocolate.

ANSWER
b. Rice. The crop that we grow the most of in the world is maize, but a lot of that is grown for feeding animals, not humans. So the most widely consumed staple food for humans is probably rice. Rice provides more than one fifth of the calories eaten worldwide by humans each day. Rice was first farmed between 13,500 and 8,200 years ago in the Pearl River valley region of China, from where it spread around the world.

2. Who invented plastic? (Andres, 6)

a. English chemist Alexander Parkes.
b. French scientist Louis Pasteur.
c. American industrialist John Wesley Hyatt.

ANSWER

c. American industrialist John Wesley Hyatt.
Hyatt invented a hard plastic called celluloid in 1869.
This material could be heated up and then moulded
into different shapes before it hardened again when it
cooled. It was made into all sorts of things, including
camera film (it was used to make very early movies),
but its downside is it catches fire easily. The English chemist Alexander Parkes created a plastic-like
material slightly earlier in the 1850s which he called
Parkesine, but this didn't become widely used.

3. What is the biggest fish? (Charlotte, 8)

a. The whale shark.
b. The basking shark.
c. The blue whale.

ANSWER

a. The whale shark. The whale shark is the largest fish on the planet – the biggest one ever measured was twelve metres long, but it is thought that
there are even bigger ones out there. You don't need
to be scared of them, though, for despite their size
they feed on plankton (tiny organisms that float
around in the sea) not people. Sometimes whale

sharks even allow swimmers to hitch a lift and be carried along with them. The basking shark is the second largest fish, and also feeds on plankton. Blue whales are the largest creatures on the planet, but they are mammals and not fish.

4. What makes an orange orange? (Pam, 7)

a. They are painted orange in the shops to make them look tasty.

b. In the Middle Ages, red and yellow lemons were cross-bred to create oranges.

c. They contain the colour pigment carotene.

ANSWER

c. They contain the colour pigment carotene. Like all orange-coloured fruit and vegetables (carrots, butternut squash) oranges contain a natural colour called carotene, which makes them orange. Oranges first grew in China, and found their way around the world via India and Persia – Arab traders brought them to Europe. These first oranges were quite bitter (like lemons), and are the kind we now use in marmalade. Sweet oranges came to Britain in the seventeenth century and were enjoyed as a snack in the theatre, much as you would eat a tub of ice cream or popcorn today.

5. How long does it take for the Earth to make a full circle? (Chloe, 10)

a. A year.

b. A day.

c. 230 million years.

d. All of the above.

ANSWER

d. All of the above. The Earth rotates in lots of ways. It spins on its own axis every twenty-four hours (a day), but takes a whole year, 365.25 days, to travel once around the Sun. At the same time, our entire solar system is busy orbiting the centre of our galaxy (the Milky Way) – and even though the solar system is travelling at 828,000 kilometres an hour, it still takes about 230 million years to get all the way round.

6. Why are reindeer called reindeer? (Hartley, 3)

a. They enjoy the rain.

b. It's a Viking word.

c. It's the Finnish word for 'Rudolf'.

b. It's a Viking word. Our word reindeer comes from the old Norse (Viking) word *hreindýri*. In America the word for reindeer is caribou. The reindeer is the only species of deer in which both males and females have antlers. Reindeer travel up to 5,000 kilometres a year, a record for mammals. They're fast, too, reaching speeds of 70 kilometres per hour (kph) on land and 10 kph in water.

7. How many strands of hair does the average person have? (Joe, 9)

a. Between 100,000 and 150,000.
b. More than a million.
c. About 50,000.

ANSWER

a. Between 100,000 and 150,000. The average person has between 100,000 and 150,000 individual hairs growing on their head at a rate of ten to thirteen millimetres a month. The person with the longest hair in the world (according to the *Guinness Book of Records*) is the Chinese lady Xie Qiuping, whose hair was 5.627 metres long when it was measured in 2004. She started growing it when she was thirteen, in 1973.

8. How many children's books did Roald Dahl write? (Habibah, 9)

a. Seventeen.

b. Four.

c. A hundred.

ANSWER

a. Seventeen. Roald Dahl wrote seventeen books of fiction (stories) for children. Try naming at least eight of them for a bonus point! They are: *The Gremlins* (1943), *James and the Giant Peach* (1961), *Charlie and the Chocolate Factory* (1964), *The Magic Finger* (1966), *Fantastic Mr Fox* (1970), *Charlie and the Great Glass Elevator* (1972), *Danny, the Champion of the World* (1975), *The Enormous Crocodile* (1978), *The Twits* (1980), *George's Marvellous Medicine* (1981), *The BFG* (1982), *The Witches* (1983), *The Giraffe and the Pelly and Me* (1985), *Matilda* (1988), *Esio Trot* (1990), *The Vicar of Nibbleswicke* (1991) and *The Minpins* (1991). He also wrote three poetry books and nine books for grown-ups.

QUIZ FOUR

1. Does the sky weigh anything? (Hany, 8)

a. No, it's just air.

b. Yes, but it depends where you are in the world.

c. Yes, about 5.5 quadrillion tonnes.

ANSWER

c. Yes, about 5.5 quadrillion tonnes. The sky, Earth's atmosphere, is made up of different gases (nitrogen, oxygen, carbon dioxide and a mixture of rare gases). These all weigh something. The total weight of the atmosphere has been calculated as about 5.5 quadrillion tonnes. That's about the same as 570,000,000,000,000 adult Indian elephants! Interestingly, air is heavier at sea level because its molecules are squeezed more tightly together by the great weight of the rest of the atmosphere pushing down on them.

2. Do sharks ever sleep? (Lucas, 5)

a. Yes, they tuck themselves into the seabed every night.

b. No, they're never actually awake.

c. They like a rest but don't sleep like we do.

c. They like a rest but don't sleep like we do. Sharks do not sleep in the way that humans do, although they do have active times and resting periods. It used to be thought that sharks had to keep swimming all the time to breathe but we now know that some sharks can rest on the seabed. Even then, if you go near them their eyes will move to follow you. Some sharks can also rest while swimming as the movements are controlled by their spine not their brain. So they can rest their brain and keep moving.

3. Where does earwax come from?
(Amelie, 9)

a. It is made by glands in the outer ear.
b. It is produced by the brain to make sure the brain doesn't fall out.
c. It is just dust and grime from the air that builds up in your ear.

a. It is made by glands in the outer ear. Earwax, or cerumen, is made by glands in the outer ear to protect the delicate skin of the ear canal from water and to stop stuff like dust, bacteria and germs from getting into the ear. Usually it gradually works its way out of the ear canal, but if too much is produced it may get stuck and need to be removed by a doctor or nurse. Never try and poke around in your own ear with your finger or a cotton bud as you may do more harm than good. Did you know that in medieval times earwax was used to colour ink for writing manuscripts?

4. What does CD-ROM stand for? (Om, 8)

a. Computer Drive Random Online Mechanism.
b. Compact Disc Read Only Memory.
c. Cylindrical Disruptive Rodent Organising Machine.

ANSWER

b. Compact Disc Read Only Memory. This means that the compact disc has information on it that your computer can read and use, but you can't change the information on the disc or record onto it. CDs are made of plastic and on one surface they have a spiral of tiny dents, which is read by a laser inside your computer.

5. What is the smallest island in the world? (Archie, 6)

a. The island of Nauru in the Pacific Ocean.

b. The Isle of Wight in the Solent.

c. The pebble in my granny's pond.

ANSWER

a. The island of Nauru in the Pacific Ocean.
There is no strict definition of when a rock actually becomes an island, but the smallest independent island nation is the island of Nauru in the Pacific. Nauru is only 21.28 kilometres square, so you could fit it into the Isle of Wight nearly eighteen times, and it is so small that it has no capital city at all.

6. Does the creature with the scientific name 'Megatherium' still exist? (Fraser, 10)

a. No, the Megatherium, or giant ground sloth, is now extinct.

b. Yes, the Megatherium can still be found on the island of Madagascar.

c. No, but scientists have recreated one from frozen DNA.

a. No, the Megatherium, or giant ground sloth, is now extinct. The Megatherium lived on the American continent during the Pliocene and Pleistocene ages (between 5.3 million years and 11,700 years ago). This animal could stand on its hind legs and when it did so could be as tall as six metres. It was a herbivore, much like elephants and rhinos today, eating vast quantities of coarse vegetation. We know this because of the large amount of fossilised Megatherium poo that has been found in caves where they used to live. The Megatherium is related to the modern-day tree sloth.

7. Why shouldn't we look at the Sun?
(Evie, 7)

a. Heat from the Sun can change the colour of your irises.
b. The intense light could damage the retinas in the back of your eyes.
c. Fire from the Sun could sear through your eyes and sizzle your brain.

ANSWER
b. The intense light could damage the retinas

in the back of your eyes. You must never look directly at the Sun (not even through sunglasses) as the light could permanently damage your retinas, the light-sensing membranes at the back of your eyes. The retina contains light-sensitive cells called cones and rods, which, in normal conditions, help you see. If you look directly at the Sun, especially for a long time, these cells can be 'cooked' and destroyed, causing a blind spot. You might not notice this damage straight away because you can't feel pain in your retina, so it wouldn't hurt.

8. Do carrots really make you see in the dark? (Sarah, 9, and Tommy, 12)

a. No, it was a story put about in the Second World War to get people to eat more carrots.
b. Yes, as long as you cut them thinly enough to see through them.
c. Yes, eating carrots gives you superhuman night vision.

ANSWER
a. No, it was a story put about in the Second World War to get people to eat more carrots. During the war a British pilot called 'Cat's

Eyes' Cunningham became the first man to shoot down a German plane at night. He became a great celebrity, and a popular myth grew up about his eating lots of carrots. The Ministry of Food deliberately encouraged this in order to get people to eat UK-grown carrots, as they were one of the few plentiful food sources at the time. In fact, carrots do contain vitamin A, which is necessary for seeing in very low light levels, though you can also get this from spinach.

QUIZ FIVE

1. How do worms breathe? (Zak, 7, and Joshua, 12)

a. They don't need to breathe as they mostly live underground.

b. They have barely visible nostrils at their front end.

c. Through their skin.

ANSWER

c. Through their skin. Earthworms take in oxygen (and let out carbon dioxide) though their skin, provided their skin is moist enough. If they dry out – in the sun for example – they die. To prevent this happening, they produce a type of slimy mucus along their body, which helps to trap the oxygen, and body fluid is released in the gaps between the segments. If the weather is very dry, worms burrow down into the ground to find moisture. If it rains very hard, though, water can take the place of oxygen in the soil and earthworms are in danger of drowning. This is why they come to the surface after a heavy rainstorm.

2. What is your body's biggest organ?
(Lewis, 10)

a. The liver.

b. The skin.

c. The brain.

ANSWER

b. The skin. Your skin counts as an organ, and is easily the largest. (The liver is the largest *internal* organ.) An average adult's skin weighs about 3.6 kilograms and would have an area of about two square metres – or at least it would if you took it off, which we don't recommend. Your skin does an amazing amount for you, as well as allowing you to feel and touch things: it is waterproof, it helps protect you from getting too hot or cold, and it stops your insides from being damaged by sunlight or nasty chemicals. It can also stop infections from getting inside the body and it makes vitamin D, which is vital to keep your bones healthy. Finally, of course, your skin holds all the rest of you together. Without it you might simply evaporate!

3. Why are catfish called catfish? (Liam, 10)

a. They have feelers which look like cats' whiskers.

b. They like eating cats.

c. When caught they make a sound very like a cat miaowing.

a. They have feelers which look like cats' whiskers. Catfish have feelers, called barbels, on either side of their mouths, which look like the whiskers of a cat. The fish use these barbels to find, touch and taste their food. There are many types of catfish. All have at least two barbels, but many species have more pairs on their nose or around their chin. Some species of catfish have been reported to be as long as 4.5 metres, but the largest one ever caught is thought to be one netted in the Mekong River in Thailand in 2010, which was 2.7 metres long and as big as a grizzly bear.

4. How do you say 1000,000,000,000,000 (the number one followed by fifteen zeros)? (Eve, 7)

a. You can't, no one has thought up a name for it yet.

b. A quadrillion.

c. A gazillion.

b. A quadrillion. The digit 1 followed by fifteen zeros is called a quadrillion and is usually written as 10^{15}, or 10 to the power of 15, which means ten times itself fifteen times. In fact, we usually write any number larger than 1,000,000 (one million) as 10 to the power of something. To get an idea of just how big a quadrillion is, if you had a stack of one quadrillion pennies, they'd reach from the Sun to the planet Jupiter and back again.

5. Do bananas have seeds? (Thea, 7)

a. No, bananas are actually animals.

b. Yes, the whole banana is a seed.

c. Yes, but you can't grow a new banana plant from them.

ANSWER

c. Yes, but you can't grow a new banana plant from them. The yellow bananas we see in shops do have seeds – the tiny black specks inside the fruit – but they are undeveloped and cannot grow. Instead the banana puts out suckers, and exact copies of the parent plant (clones) can grow from these. Because they are clones they cannot evolve resistance to diseases, so they are very vulnerable. Wild banana varieties can still produce seeds, however.

6. Which actor was the first to play James Bond? (Fergus, 9)

a. Daniel Craig.
b. Sean Connery.
c. Barry Nelson.

ANSWER

c. Barry Nelson. Even though Sean Connery was the first James Bond in a cinema film (he was in *Dr No*, which was made in 1962), the American actor Barry Nelson played James 'Jimmy' Bond in a black-and-white 1954 TV adaptation of Ian Fleming's novel *Casino Royale*, in which the British secret agent was recast as an American.

7. What is salt? (Juhi, 8)

a. Mermaid dandruff.
b. Dried-out hail.
c. Sodium chloride.

c. Sodium chloride. Table salt, the stuff we use on our food, is a substance called sodium chloride, the result of a chemical reaction between the elements sodium and chlorine. Salt is taken from the sea or from salt springs (when the water in the sea evaporates, we are left with salt) or it can be mined. In fact most of the salt we add to our food has been dug out from the earth. Salt is also used on our roads in the winter as it helps stop water turning into ice when it is very cold.

8. What is the world's longest song?
(Jasmine, 8)

a. 'Bohemian Rhapsody' by Queen.
b. 'Longplayer' by Jem Finer.
c. An Aboriginal folk song.

ANSWER

b. 'Longplayer' by Jem Finer. There are a number of pop songs that are over twenty minutes long but that's nothing compared to 'Organ^2/ASLSP (As SLow aS Possible)', by John Cage. The current performance of the piece began in 2001 in a church in Germany and is meant to go on for 639 years, ending in the year 2640. But even that is short compared to 'Longplayer', which began playing at midnight on 31 December 1999 and will continue to play without repetition until the last moment of the year 2999. Then it will begin its cycle again. 'Longplayer' is composed for singing bowls – an ancient type of standing bell – which can be played by both humans and machines.

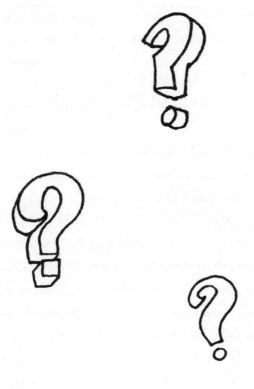

QUIZ SIX

1. Can dogs see in colour? (Amber, 8)

a. Yes, their eyes are just like ours.
b. No, they see everything in black and white.
c. Yes, but only in a limited way.

ANSWER

c. Yes, but only in a limited way. Dogs are not completely colourblind but they don't see colours as well as we do. This is because humans have three types of colour receptor cells in our eyes, for red, green and blue light. Dogs only have two types of sensor, for yellow and blue. This does not mean that dogs can't see green or red objects. It only means that they can't tell the difference between green, yellow or red objects based on their colour, so they see colours in a similar way to how a red-green colourblind human does. Some animals have much better colour vision than humans. Some birds have four different types of colour receptor, some fish have five and the mantis shrimp has twelve!

2. What makes fireworks bang? (James, 5)

a. A pixie with a drum inside the firework.
b. Clappers inside the firework hitting each other.
c. The sudden expansion of gas in the firework.

ANSWER

c. The sudden expansion of gas in the firework. The bang when a firework goes off is caused by a pressure wave. When you light a firework the solid explosive burns rapidly, making a lot of gas. This gas expands very quickly, pushing against the air around it to create a pressure wave. When this pressure wave hits our ears we hear a 'bang'.

3. At what time of day is your shadow longest? (Harvey, 7)

a. In the middle of the night.
b. At the beginning or end of the day.
c. In the middle of the day.

ANSWER

b. At the beginning or end of the day. Your shadow is at its longest when the Sun is at its lowest on the horizon, so either at the very beginning of the day when the Sun is rising or at the very end of the day when it is setting. In the middle of the day your shadow is at its shortest because the Sun is right above you. If you were standing on the equator at exactly midday, the Sun would be directly over your head and you wouldn't have a shadow at all.

4. Was Vincent Van Gogh famous when he was alive? (Chloe, 7)

a. No, he only sold one painting when he was alive.
b. Yes, he was a multimillionaire by the time he died.
c. Yes, but only in Japan.

ANSWER

a. No, he only sold one painting when he was alive. Vincent Van Gogh, now thought to be one of the best Dutch painters ever, led a troubled life. His younger brother, Theo, who was a picture dealer in Paris, supported him and often sent him money and art materials. Vincent killed himself in 1890, having created over 800 oil paintings and 700 drawings. In 1990, 100 years after it was painted, his *Portrait of Dr Gachet* was sold for $82.5 million, making it one of the most expensive paintings ever.

5. What is glass made from? (Harini and Andres, 6)

a. Frozen water.
b. Sand.
c. Diamonds cut really thinly.

ANSWER

b. Sand. You can make glass just from melting sand but you have to heat it to a very high temperature. A chemical called sodium carbonate is therefore added to the sand to make it melt at a lower temperature, which is easier to manage. However, glass made with just sand and sodium carbonate easily dissolves in water, which wouldn't be much use. Just imagine drinking from a glass that dissolved in water! So lime (the mineral, not the fruit) is added too, and this makes a usable glass.

6. How do snails eat? (Jacob, 10)

a. They spit poison onto the food, which dissolves it, then they suck it up.
b. They have teeth like us and chew their food before swallowing it.
c. They shred their food and then pass it into their mouth.

c. They shred their food and then pass it into their mouth. Snails shred their food using a ribbon-shaped organ called a radula which has rows of 'teeth' on it. The food is then passed into the mouth rather like a conveyor belt. Slugs feed in the same way, and are just like snails except that they are covered with a layer of slimy mucus instead of a shell.

7. What is the smallest bone in the human body? (Skye, 9)

a. The stapes, in your ear.
b. The distal phalanx, in your little finger.
c. Your coccyx.

ANSWER

a. The stapes, in your ear. The stapes (or stirrup), at only three millimetres long, is the smallest bone in your body. It is one of three tiny bones in your middle ear which form a kind of chain to transmit sound waves picked up by your ear drum to the liquid of your inner ear. The other two bones are called the malleus (or hammer) and the incus (or anvil). The bones at the very tips of your fingers are called distal phalanges and while they are pretty small they are several times bigger than your stapes.

8. Why is the planet Mars red?
(Armondo, 11)

a. It's not really red, it is just surrounded by reddish gases which make it look red from Earth.
b. It is boiling hot.
c. Its surface contains a lot of iron.

ANSWER

c. Its surface contains a lot of iron. The crust of Mars contains a large amount of iron, which makes it red in colour. (That's also why rust is red, and your blood too.) You can see the Red Planet, as it is sometimes called, from Earth. The hottest it gets on Mars is about twenty degrees Celsius, at noon at the equator, but it can be as cold as minus 153 at the poles. It can also be extremely windy. Sometimes wind storms can be so huge they cover the whole planet and it can take months for the dust to settle.

QUIZ SEVEN

1. In *Peter Pan*, what was Captain Hook's name before he got his hand bitten off? (Amos, 5)

a. Able Seaman Hook.
b. Captain Hand.
c. We don't know.

ANSWER

c. We don't know. J. M. Barrie, the author who created Captain James Hook, tells us that the pirate villain got his name when Peter Pan cut his hand off and fed it to a crocodile, which meant he had to replace it with a hook. He doesn't, however, reveal what Hook's name was before this happened, telling us that 'Hook was not his true name. To reveal who he really was would even at this date set the country in a blaze.' So it is too dangerous for us to know!

2. How do earthquakes happen? (Utbah, 8)

a. Earthquakes are caused by too many people jumping up and down at the same time.

b. Earthquakes are caused by rocky plates rubbing together.

c. Earthquakes happen when the Earth gets too close to the Sun.

ANSWER

b. Earthquakes are caused by rocky plates rubbing together. The Earth's crust is made up of a series of vast rocky 'plates'. Although we can't feel it, these plates are moving very slowly all the time – just a few millimetres or centimetres a year each. The edges of these plates are not smooth, so where they meet tension can build up as they grind against each other. This tension can suddenly be released, causing the ground to shake in an earthquake.

3. What are comets made from?
(Catriona, 9)

a. Dust and ice.
b. Fire.
c. Broken spaceships.

ANSWER

a. Dust and ice. A comet is made up of dust and ice, like a dirty snowball. When a comet gets near the Sun, the ice heats up so much it turns into a gas and, mixed up with dust, forms a kind of atmosphere around the comet which is called a 'coma'. The stream of particles that is always coming off the Sun, called the 'solar wind', blows this atmosphere out into a tail, which always points away from the Sun. The ancient Greeks thought this looked hairy, so they called them *kometes* (Ancient Greek for 'long-haired'). That's why we call them comets.

4. Why is poo always brown, even when you eat all your veg? (Amelia, 7)

a. It shows you are eating too much chocolate.
b. That's the colour of the worn-out red blood cells in your poo.
c. All colours mixed together always end up brown.

ANSWER
b. That's the colour of the worn-out red blood cells in your poo. When the red cells in your blood get worn out and can't do their job properly any more, your body has to get rid of them. They turn a brownish colour and come out in your poo, making it brown. If these old blood cells are unable to enter your intestine (which happens if you have

a condition called obstructive jaundice), your poo can actually become much paler or even white.

5. Why do people shrink when they're old? (Shazra, 9)

a. The squishy discs between the vertebrae (back bones) shrink.
b. Your leg bones start to contract as you get old.
c. Other people are not really shrinking, you're just growing taller.

ANSWER
a. The squishy discs between the vertebrae (back bones) shrink. Between each of the bones in your back, called vertebrae, there is a squishy jelly-like disc that acts like a cushion. These cushions get squashed during the day, losing water, which means that at the end of the day everyone is a bit shorter (up to 1.9 centimetres) than they were at the beginning of the day (even you!). When you go to bed and lie down this takes the pressure off the discs and they get nice and plump again so that you are back to your normal height in the morning. This doesn't happen so easily in old people's bodies, so they stay a bit shorter and start shrinking;

some people can be five centimetres shorter by the time they are sixty years old.

6. Which animals that are alive today evolved from dinosaurs? (Jake, 10)

a. Crocodiles.

b. Ants.

c. Birds.

ANSWER

c. Birds. One branch of the therapod dinosaur family (the group that includes Tyrannosaurus Rex) contained the ancestors of modern birds, so birds are actually surviving dinosaurs. All the other dinosaurs became extinct around 65 million years ago. Modern crocodiles are descended from a different type of prehistoric reptile, not in the dinosaur family.

7. Why is the Sun yellow? (Shannea, 10)

a. It isn't, it's white.

b. It's made of yellow gases.

c. Yellow is the most cheerful colour.

a. It isn't, it's white. The Sun is a ball of gas which produces light of all the colours of the rainbow. Mixed together, these colours make white light, and that is the 'colour' of sunlight. Indeed, when seen from space the Sun is white. However, most of the blue rays from the Sun's rays are filtered out by Earth's atmosphere, so we don't see them – we see more of the yellow-green light rays and that's why the Sun looks yellow to us. When the Sun is rising or setting and is low in the sky, its light has to pass through more atmosphere to reach us, and then it often looks more orange or even red.

8. Why do we sweat when we're hot?
(Mia, 8)

a. To cool ourselves down.
b. To make ourselves look nice and shiny.
c. To scare away pests.

ANSWER

a. To cool ourselves down. When we get hot, sweat is released by our sweat glands onto our skin. Then the heat from our body makes the sweat evaporate, which cools down our skin. We also sweat sometimes when our body is fighting an infection — our temperature rises and the sweat glands start working to cool us down. If we are feeling nervous or excited we sweat too, but not all over. If we are sweating because of worry, we are more likely to have sweaty palms, feet, forehead or underarms.

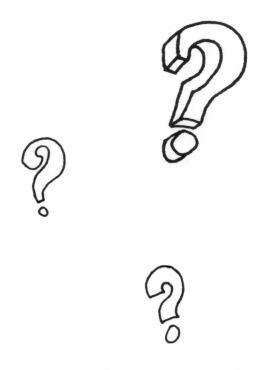

QUIZ EIGHT

1. If a snake bites itself can it poison itself? (Lewis, 10)

a. Yes, so they have to be very careful.

b. Yes, but when they do they don't die, they just lose their skin.

c. No, a snake is immune to its own venom.

ANSWER

c. No, a snake is immune to its own venom. Although it is extremely unlikely that a snake would be silly enough to bite itself, it seems snakes have immunity to their own venom. What is more, snakes can choose *not* to release venom when they bite (this is called a 'dry bite'). So if a snake did end up biting itself for some strange reason, it would probably not release any venom anyway. Snakes shed their skin when they have outgrown it. This is a natural process and has nothing to do with venom.

2. Why do animals have tails? (Felicity, 3)

a. To help them move and balance.

b. To help them communicate.

c. All of the above.

ANSWER

c. All of the above. Tails have all sorts of uses. Fish use their tails to help them swim, and birds use their tail feathers to help them fly. Animals that climb, like squirrels or cats, use their tails to help them balance (monkeys use them like a fifth limb), and other animals use their tails to communicate. Dogs wag their tails to say they're happy, and rattlesnakes wave theirs as a warning. Tails can also swish away flies (horses and cows do this) or be used as weapons (crocodiles and alligators can do a lot of damage with their strong tails). Some lizards even use their tails to help them escape: if a predator grabs their tail, it simply snaps off, allowing the lizard to run away.

3. What are black holes? (Toby, 6)

a. Places behind the sofa where lost socks go.

b. Another name for craters on the Moon.

c. Areas in space where gravity is unbelievably strong.

c. Areas in space where gravity is unbelievably strong. A black hole is an object that has so much matter in such a small space that its gravity is strong enough to prevent light or anything else from escaping. They form when a huge star collapses in on itself. As they even suck light in, we can't see them, but we know they exist as we can see material being pulled in by their huge gravitational field. There are billions of black holes in the Universe but none of them is near enough for us to worry about.

4. Why do our tears taste salty? (Daniel, 6)

a. To stop you drinking them.
b. To help them run smoothly down your face.
c. To keep your eyes healthy.

ANSWER

c. To keep your eyes healthy. Your eyes are always bathed in a salty liquid we call tears to keep them healthy and working properly. Your tears also contain proteins and enzymes, which help keep your eyeballs clean and moving smoothly. You may not realise it, but your eyes are producing tears all the time (150 to 300 millilitres every day). Like tears, all the liquids that come out of your body are slightly salty, including your blood and your wee.

5. Why is the sea blue on a sunny day?
(Jessica, 9)

a. Because of all the blue fish in it.
b. Because the sea reflects more blue light than any other colour.
c. Because the bottom of the sea is blue.

ANSWER

b. Because the sea reflects more blue light than any other colour. The light from the Sun is made up of all the colours (and appears white), but when it shines on the sea, the red, green, orange and yellow light sinks in while the blue and violet light is bounced back. This blue and violet light is what we see, so the sea looks blue to us, though of course we know that water itself is transparent. Sometimes sea water can look brown if there is silt in it, or green if it contains algae.

6. Does lightning ever hit cows? (Isaac, 8)

a. Yes, but they are never hurt because they are fully insulated.

b. No, they stay inside during storms.

c. Yes, lightning will hit anything in its path.

ANSWER

c. Yes, lightning will hit anything in its path. If a cow is caught out in an electric storm, it is just as likely to be hit as you are – if there is nothing taller nearby which can conduct electricity. There is a theory that animals with all four feet on the ground are more likely to be electrocuted during a storm, as two of their feet will be on the ground closer to the strike point and the other two a bit further away. This lets the electric current from the lightning pass through their body more easily.

7. What was the 2012 Olympic mascot? (Kieron, 10)

a. A droplet of steel from the building of the Olympic stadium called Wenlock.

b. A British lion called Pride.

c. The Friendlies.

a. A droplet of steel from the building of the Olympic stadium called Wenlock. The official mascot featured in a story by children's author Michael Morpurgo, in which he was created from a droplet of steel during the building of the stadium. He was named Wenlock after the Shropshire town of Much Wenlock, where an early version of the modern Olympic Games took place. The Paralympic mascot was Mandeville, named after Stoke Mandeville in Buckinghamshire, where the Paralympic Games began. Both mascots had a single large camera-lens eye, a London taxi lamp on their heads and Olympic Rings bracelets around their wrists. Pride the lion was the Team GB mascot, and the Friendlies were the mascots for the 2008 Games in Beijing, China.

8. Why do people have different eye colours? (Constance, 9)

a. To make us look nice.

b. Because of different amounts of colour pigment in our eyes.

c. It depends on where you're born.

b. Because of different amounts of colour pigment in our eyes. The coloured part of your eye is a muscle called the iris, which controls the amount of light getting in through a hole in the middle called your pupil. Your iris contains a certain amount of the coloured pigment melatonin (which is responsible for the colour of your skin and hair as well) and it is the exact amount and distribution of this melatonin that determines your eye colour. If you have lots of melatonin you will have darker, brown eyes and if you have very little or none at all you will have very light eyes which appear blue. Between these two extremes are all the other colours your eyes could be: green, hazel, amber, grey or violet.

CONTRIBUTORS

Jim Al-Khalili (pp. 36, 180, 215) is a British scientist, author and broadcaster. He is a professor of physics at the University of Surrey and enjoys helping people understand science.

Alexander Armstrong (pp. xiii, 229) is a comedian, actor and TV presenter. He's one half of comedy duo Armstrong and Miller and hosts the popular quiz show *Pointless*. With Richard Osman, he's the author of *The 100 Most Pointless Things in the World*.

David Attenborough (p. 3) is Britain's best known natural history film-maker and environmentalist. His career as a naturalist and broadcaster has spanned nearly five decades and there are very few places on the globe that he hasn't visited.

Iain Logie Baird (p. 222) is the grandson of John Logie Baird who invented the television. Iain is interested in pictures, wires and fixing things, too. He's an associate curator at the National Media Museum in Bradford, England, where he helps take care of the National Television Collection.

Johnny Ball (p. 204) has been a lively enthuser about maths and science since the 1960s. A regular on children's

287

TV shows, he's fronted, among others, *Think of a Number*. Johnny continues to solve life's puzzles in his latest book, *Ball of Confusion*. He's much-loved Dad to radio DJ and presenter, Zoe.

Patrick Barkham (p. 110) grew up in the Norfolk countryside. He has written a book about hunting for butterflies called *The Butterfly Isles* and a book about badgers called *Badgerlands*. He is now writing a book about why we love the seaside.

Simon Baron-Cohen (p. 90) has been amazed by the human brain since he was a little boy. He's director of the Autism Research Centre at Cambridge University and author of *Zero Degrees of Empathy*. He's also cousin to Ali G actor Sacha Baron-Cohen.

Paul Barrett (pp. 76, 155) is the dinosaur expert at the Natural History Museum, London. He studied at Cambridge University and had jobs there and at Oxford University before arriving at the museum. He's travelled all over the world to study dinosaurs, especially China, Australia, South Africa and the USA.

Alex Bellos (p. 60) is the author of *Alex's Adventures in Numberland,* a book about why maths is fun and relevant to the real world. He has lived in Brazil and written about its favourite sport in a book called *Futebol.*

David Bellos (p. 197) has a keen interest in languages and the different ways that we speak. He writes books with cool titles, like *Is That a Fish in Your Ear?* The rest of the time he teaches at Princeton University in the USA, and is delighted to be dad of the above.

Quentin Blake (p. 44) drew the brilliant illustrations in your Roald Dahl books. He's been drawing for as long as he can remember, and recently launched *Beyond the Page*, a book about what it's like to be an illustrator, to celebrate his eightieth birthday. He merrily admits to a freewheeling style.

Heston Blumenthal (p. 107) is the chef who invented snail porridge and bacon-and-egg ice cream. He taught himself to cook, and likes experimenting with unusual flavours and techniques. A bit like Willy Wonka.

William Boyd (p. 68) has often imagined what it's like to be a spy through his novels and screenplays. Now he's taken on 007 by writing a James Bond sequel, called *Solo*. He is perhaps best known for his novel *Any Human Heart*, which was recently adapted for television.

Derren Brown (p. 7) is a performer who combines magic and psychology to seemingly predict and control human behaviour, as well as achieving mind-bending feats of mentalism. He also writes books, paints portraits and has a deep love for parrots.

Oliver Burkeman (p. 80) is a writer for the *Guardian* newspaper, based in New York. His latest book, *The Antidote: Happiness for People Who Can't Stand Positive Thinking*, explores the good things that can come out of uncertainty, failure and imperfection.

Ellie Cannon (p. 5) is a GP and TV doctor who writes a weekly column in the *Mail on Sunday* newspaper. She once delivered a woman's baby on the toilet floor of her doctor's surgery because she didn't have time to get her to the hospital!

Helen Castor (p. 211) loves writing about people from the olden days, particularly queens. She presents Radio 4's *Making History* programme every week and her book *She-Wolves* was made into a three-part series for BBC Four.

Noam Chomsky (p. 33) is a linguist and philosopher based at the Massachusetts Institute of Technology, in the USA.

Marcus Chown (pp. 13, 195) writes books for grown-ups on things like black holes and the Big Bang, and very silly books for children, such as *Felicity Frobisher and the Three-Headed Aldebaran Dust Devil*.

Brian Clegg (pp. 62, 124) studied physics at Cambridge University. He used to work at British Airways, finding new technology for the airline, but for more than ten years he has been writing books about the bits of science he finds exciting, like how to build a time machine, the science inside our bodies and infinity.

Quentin Cooper (pp. 51, 173) is regularly referred to as 'the world's most enthusiastic man', so great is his love for both science and the arts. He writes for newspapers and magazines, speaks at science festivals and events, and is best known for presenting BBC Radio 4's most listened-to science programme *Material World*.

Heather Couper (pp. 78, 167) is a broadcaster and author on astronomy and space. She ran the Greenwich Planetarium for five years and has written over thirty books. In 1986 she was the astronomer onboard Concorde when it flew from London to New Zealand, showing the passengers Halley's Comet. Asteroid number 3922 is named 'Heather' in her honour.

Brian Cox (p. 2) is a particle physicist, science presenter and former pop star who makes physics fun. If you're fascinated by space and the natural world, you'll probably have seen him in *Stargazing Live* and *Wonders of Life*. When he's not making TV and writing books, he teaches at Manchester University and works on experiments at the Large Hadron Collider at CERN in Switzerland.

David Crystal (p. 185) has been described as a mixture of Gandalf and Dumbledore, thanks to his big white beard. In fact he is a professor who writes books and gives talks about the languages of the world.

Helen Czerski (p. 92) asked lots of questions about the world when she was a child. Now she's a physicist she knows some of the answers! She's often on telly and radio programmes like Dara Ó Briain's *Science Club* and *Horizon* on the BBC, and Radio 4's *Museum of Curiosity*. Helen loves science, badminton and hot chocolate, and is an expert on the tiny bubbles you find on ocean waves.

Ken Denmead (p. 19) is a husband and father from the San Francisco Bay Area, where he works as the editorial director for Maker Media. He's also the publisher of Geek-Dad, a parenting blog where, along with other dedicated geeky parents, he posts projects, reviews and podcasts about being a parent and being a geek.

Lee Dixon (p. 11) played right back for Arsenal, Burnley, Bury, Chester City and Stoke City football teams as well as the England national team. While at Arsenal he collected four League champion's medals, three FA Cup Winner's medals and a UEFA Cup Winners' Cup medal.

Since retiring, he has become a football analyst for ITV Sport and raises funds for charities like Sport Relief.

Caitlin Doughty (p. 159) is a mortician and writer living in Los Angeles. She is the host of the 'Ask a Mortician' webseries and the founder of the Order of the Good Death, a group of artists, academics and funeral professionals dedicated to changing how we look at death.

Marcus du Sautoy (p. 149) is a professor of mathematics at the University of Oxford. His many programmes about maths include *The Code* and some with comedians Alan Davies and Dara Ó Briain. He has also worked with Lauren Child (creator of *Charlie and Lola*), providing puzzles and codes for her books about child spy Ruby Redfort.

Daphne J. Fairbairn (p. 115) has always loved studying animals in their natural environments, and has worked with mice, insects and spiders. Early in her career she was inspired to research the differences between males and females in species – an area that has held her attention ever since. Daphne's new book is *Odd Couples: Extraordinary Differences between the Sexes in the Animal Kingdom*.

Charles Fernyhough (p. 157) is a writer and psychologist based at Durham University. He wrote a book, *The Baby in the Mirror*, about his daughter Athena's first three years. He also has a little boy, Isaac, who likes cricket, drumming, wrestling, drawing and animals.

William Fiennes (p. 132) was very ill in his twenties. He found comfort in books about birds and developed a fascination with geese. When he recovered, he packed his bags and went on a 2,000-mile journey to watch them migrate, then wrote a beautiful book about it called *The Snow Geese*.

Joshua Foer (p. 101) has written a book called *Moonwalking with Einstein*, all about the potential of the human brain. He can often be found pondering life's wonders at his online compendium, Atlas Obscura.

Kevin Fong (p. 226) is a doctor of medicine, with expertise in space medicine. He likes to explore how the body manages in extreme conditions – from travelling in the Antarctic to a mission to Mars. His new book is called *Extremes: Life, Death and the Limits of the Human Body*.

Greg Foot (pp. 53, 108) has been buried, frozen and electrocuted, all in the name of science. A daredevil science presenter, Greg can be seen performing science stunts on TV, unpicking interesting science questions on YouTube and presenting live science shows at schools and festivals.

Alys Fowler (pp. 34, 143) loves gardening and so does her dog, Isobel. (Though sometimes Isobel digs holes in the wrong place and Alys finds dog bones among the parsnips.) Trained in horticulture, she appears on gardening shows and writes books and columns.

Douglas D. Gaffin (p. 86) is a professor in the biology department at the University of Oklahoma. His research focuses on understanding the special sensory abilities of scorpions and other arthropods. In his spare time, he enjoys volleyball, camping, biking, hiking and playing the banjo.

Paul Geraghty (p. 32) is author and illustrator of *Dinosaur in Danger* and many other books. He grew up in South

Africa and now travels the world in search of stories and the words with which to tell them, having close encounters with many animals along the way. He also does head-melting sessions at schools.

Philip Gooden (pp. 121, 171) writes books on language, including *Who's Whose?* and *The Story of English*, as well as mystery novels set in the age of Shakespeare. He blogs occasionally on words on his website.

A. C. Grayling (pp. 15, 179) is Master of the New College of the Humanities in London. He has written and edited over twenty books on philosophy and other subjects. Anthony ran away from school when he was fourteen, in protest at being caned too much, and is very glad that the cane is not used any more.

John and Mary Gribbin (pp. 56, 74) write books about science for young readers. John used to be an astronomer and Mary used to be a teacher. They try out their ideas on their granddaughter Bella and grandson William.

Bear Grylls (p. 18) has eaten maggots and slept in a deer carcass for his TV series *Man vs Wild* and *Born Survivor*. Trained in martial arts as a boy, he went on to join the British Special Forces and climbed Everest at just twenty-three. Bear has led many expeditions for charity in faraway places from Antarctica to the Arctic, and is Chief Scout in the UK.

John Gurdon (p. 85) is a biologist, well known for his pioneering research in nuclear transplantation and cloning. In 2012 he was awarded the Nobel Prize for his stem cell research.

Celia Haddon (p. 137) is the author of *Cats Behaving Badly* and *One Hundred Ways for a Cat to Train Its Human*. She recently wrote the biography of her current pet, *Tilly the Ugliest Cat in the Shelter*.

Claudia Hammond (p. 187) is a broadcaster, writer and psychology lecturer. She's written two books: *Time Warped* and *Emotional Rollercoaster* – a journey through the science of feelings. Claudia presents *All in the Mind* and *Mind Changers* on BBC Radio 4 and *Health Check* on BBC World Service.

Tim Harford (p. 88) writes books about economic ideas in everyday life, and he also writes for the *Financial Times* newspaper. He presents a BBC radio show, *More or Less*, about how to tell when numbers are lying to us.

Dawn Harper (pp. 98, 131) is a GP. She is often seen helping people with their embarrassing health problems on *Embarrassing Bodies*, but can also be found on the sofa of ITV's *This Morning*.

Miranda Hart (p. 30) is a comedy writer and actress whose sitcom *Miranda* has made her one of Britain's favourite comedians. She wanted to be in comedy since she could remember but is not giving up on her other dream: to be Wimbledon Ladies' Champion.

Adam Hart-Davis (p. 96) is a writer and former TV presenter. He has read several books and written about thirty. His latest is a colourful pop-up book called *Inventions: A History of Key Inventions that Changed the World*. Adam enjoys woodwork and spends a lot of time making chairs, egg cups and spoons.

Rob Hicks (pp. 119, 191) is a doctor, health writer, author and medical adviser for the BBC. He's often on telly and radio: a regular on 5 Live and ITV's *This Morning*. He also cycles and sings in a rock band that's about to record its first album.

Tom Holland (p. 104) writes books about exciting times in history. They include *Rubicon*, about the Roman Empire, and *Persian Fire*, about wars between Greece and Persia in around 500 BC. His latest, *In the Shadow of the Sword*, is about the end of those empires and the growth of Islam.

Bettany Hughes (p. 83) is a historian who's fascinated by very old civilisations, particularly Ancient Greece. She's written books on Helen of Troy and the great thinker Socrates (*The Hemlock Cup*). She makes TV programmes about all the stuff she really loves, from goddesses to gorgeous bits of old rubbish in the ground.

Kate Humble (p. 45) is a TV presenter for wildlife and science programmes. She learned to ride at the age of five and spent most of her early years mucking out horses. When not filming lions in Africa or lambing in Wales, she runs courses on countryside skills with her husband on their farm.

Julian Hume (p. 64) began his career as an artist recreating lost worlds. He became so interested in extinct animals that he trained as a scientist so that he could study them in more detail. He is now a palaeontologist and an artist all in one.

Madhur Jaffrey (p. 217) has written many bestselling books about Indian food in more than thirty years as a food writer. Her BBC TV show, *Madhur Jaffrey's Indian Cookery*, has helped make her a household name. She also acts and has appeared in many films including Merchant Ivory's *Heat and Dust*.

Karen James (p. 54) is a biologist at Mount Desert Island Biological Laboratory in Bar Harbor in Maine in the USA. She is co-founder and director of the HMS *Beagle* Project, which aims to rebuild and sail the ship that carried Charles Darwin around the world in the 1830s.

Alok Jha (p. 224) likes answering questions almost as much as asking them. He studied physics at university because he wanted to know what atoms were made of and now spends his time writing about everything from space to dinosaurs for the *Guardian* newspaper. He also presents science programmes on BBC TV and radio.

Tony Juniper (p. 209) is an environmental campaigner and writer. He helps companies and others to develop nature-friendly policies and raises awareness about the need to protect nature.

Annabel Karmel (p. 71) is an expert on what to feed babies and children, and mother of three herself. She wrote her popular *Complete Baby & Toddler Meal Planner* twenty-one years ago and has published twenty-seven more books since, as well as presenting *Annabel's Kitchen* on TV.

Sam Kean (pp. 24, 117) is the US-based author of two bestselling books, *The Violinist's Thumb*, about the hidden history buried in our DNA, and *The Disappearing Spoon*, a romp through the periodic table. He wishes he had a sports team he was passionate about, though he does love track and field.

Martin Kemp (p. 61) is a professor of art history at Oxford University. He is a world expert on that brilliant artist, inventor, engineer, musician and mathematician Leonardo da Vinci. Martin's most recent book, *Christ to Coke*, looks at how an image becomes an icon.

Simon King (p. 82) is a naturalist, author and broadcaster, best known for *Springwatch* and *Big Cat Diary*. If he were an animal he'd like to be a peregrine falcon, because flying at 1,000 feet at 200 miles per hour has to be a wonderful way to start the day.

Carol Klein (p. 41) can often be found pottering around her beautiful cottage garden in Devon, England. She's written lots of books about how to grow your own fruit and veg, and is a regular on the popular BBC *Gardeners' World* programme.

Simon Kuper (p. 109) writes for the *Financial Times* newspaper and is author of *Soccernomics* and *Football Against the Enemy*. When he was eight years old, he obviously wanted to be a professional footballer.

John Lanchester (p. 16) writes novels and non-fiction. He investigated the global financial crisis in his book *Whoops!: Why Everyone Owes Everyone and No One Can Pay*. He is contributing editor to the *London Review of Books*. London-based, John was born in Hamburg and brought up in Hong Kong.

Louise Leakey (p. 202) comes from a long line of palaeontologists. (You could say bones are in her bones!) She spent her childhood running around the deserts of northern Kenya and at age six became the youngest person to find a hominoid fossil – a 17-million-year-old ape. Today she still explores fossil remains, going back 4 million years.

Steve Leonard (p. 220) made his name as a TV vet on *Vet School* and has gone on to present wildlife series such as *Steve Leonard's Extreme Animals*, *Animal Kingdom* and *Safari Vet School*. He still can't believe his luck at getting so close to amazing animals in the wild.

Jack Lewis (p. 42) loves to explore the human brain and how it affects the senses. When he's not researching what makes us tick, he's creating a new series for the Discovery Networks.

Gareth Malone (p. 114) presented the TV series *The Choir* which reignited popular interest in classical music and received critical acclaim for inspiring so many people to get involved in choral singing. Gareth was awarded an OBE in recognition of his services to music. He lives in London with his wife and family.

Gary Marcus (p. 125) is a professor of psychology and director of the NYU Center for Language and Music. He blogs for the *New Yorker*, and his books about the origins and development of mind and brain include *The Birth of the Mind*, *Kluge* and *Guitar Zero*, described as 'Jimi Hendrix meets Oliver Sacks'. He is also a proud new dad.

Jenny Marder (p. 102) is a science editor and producer for the PBS NewsHour in the United States. She likes to tackle the big questions about science and technology, and especially enjoys writing about brains, bugs and space flight.

Zuzana Matyasova (p. 175) looks after all the birds at ZSL London Zoo. She spends a lot of her time working at Penguin

Beach with more than fifty penguins from three different species, and is very busy as they all compete for attention.

Paul McCartney (p. 21) was in a band you may have heard of called . . . the Beatles! The original boy band found fame in the 1960s, singing about yellow submarines, walruses and skies filled with diamonds, and their music is still going strong half a century later. These days Sir Paul is a solo artist and works very hard for charity.

Kevin McCloud (p. 163) is presenter of the popular programme *Grand Designs*. He is the author of eleven books, the most recent being *43 Principles of Home* and *The Best of Grand Designs*. His favourite hideaway is a cabin in the woods, which he built with his own hands.

George McGavin (pp. 22, 182, 200) has had a lifelong obsession with wildlife, particularly insects. A leading entomologist (insect expert) and zoologist, he has written numerous books and after a long university career, he now presents science and natural history programmes for the BBC. George has several insect species named after him, and hopes they survive him.

Aggie MacKenzie (p. 127) first came to our screens as Dirt Detective in Channel 4's *How Clean Is Your House?*. She's now helping the nation declutter in ITV's *Storage Hoarders* – fascinating people, stories and stuff. Aggie also writes regularly in several women's magazines.

Ben Miller (p. 28) is a comedian and actor, one half of comedy duo Armstrong and Miller (*see also* Alexander Armstrong). He's also a bona fide science geek and has written the excellent book *It's Not Rocket Science*.

Mark Miodownik (p. 169) likes making things and explaining how they work. As a scientist and engineer, he appears on TV, including the BBC's *How It Works* series in 2012. He also teaches and conducts research as Professor of Materials at University College London.

Radha Modgil (p. 136) is a doctor, TV presenter and health columnist who has appeared on many shows, including C4's *The Sex Education Show* and BBC's *Make My Body Younger*. Most recently she's been working on a show about how to deal with spots called *Body Beautiful*.

Patrick Morrow (p. 147) is a Canadian mountain climber and photographer. He began his travel adventures in an old green van over forty years ago, and has now climbed the highest mountain on every continent in the world. He's written books called *Beyond Everest: Quest for the Seven Summits* and *Everest: High Expectations*.

Jojo Moyes (p. 73) used to type braille for blind people and work as a minicab controller, before becoming a journalist at the *Independent* newspaper. She now writes best-selling novels, including *The Girl You Left Behind* and *Me Before You*. She lives on a farm in Essex with her husband and three children.

James Nestor (p. 112) spends most days in the ocean and most nights writing about it for *Outside Magazine*, *Men's Journal*, the *New York Times* and more. His book *DEEP*, which explores the sea from the surface to the lowest natural point on the planet, will be published in April 2014.

Bill Oddie (p. 69) knows lots about birds and loves watching them. He's very good at presenting wildlife shows on the telly, like *Springwatch*, and writes some rather lovely books. He can sing and play the drums and saxophone too.

Neil Oliver (p. 134) is an archaeologist and historian. He has become a familiar face presenting the BBC's *Coast* and other programmes, and his most recent book is *Vikings: A History*. Neil is happiest digging holes or watching *Indiana Jones* films.

Matt Parker (p. 161) makes maths funny. He's based at Queen Mary, University of London, but when he's not lecturing about numbers, he's also a stand-up comedian. You can hear him on BBC Radio 4's *Infinite Monkey Cage*.

Jeremy Paxman (p. 23) asks lots of hard questions on *Newsnight* and *University Challenge*, and makes very good history documentaries too. To wind down, he enjoys fly fishing.

Max Pemberton (p. 105) is a doctor, journalist and writer. He is a columnist for the *Daily Telegraph* and for *Reader's Digest*, and writes for the *Mail on Sunday*. He has also written three books, the most recent being *The Doctor Will See You Now*.

Justin Pollard (p. 37) is a historian who spends most of his time writing books, articles and TV shows such as *QI*. He has advised on movies from *The Boy in the Striped Pyjamas* to *Pirates of the Caribbean* and has also written nine books, one with an exploding toilet in it.

Maria Popova (p. 151) is the founder and editor of Brain Pickings (brainpickings.org), where she catalogues interesting bits across art, science, history, philosophy and more. She has written for the *New York Times*, *Wired* UK,

The Atlantic, Harvard's *Nieman Reports*, and *Smithsonian Magazine*, among others, and is an MIT Fellow. She spends lots of time on Twitter as @brainpicker.

Mark Porter (p. 213) spends half his week at his GP surgery in the Cotswolds and the other half writing and talking about medical matters for *The Times*, Radio 4 and *The One Show*. Here he's written about taste buds. (His favourite taste is sweet, what's yours?)

Christopher Riley (pp. 140, 177) is a writer, broadcaster and film-maker specialising in astronomy and space flight. He has floated weightless on Russian and European space agency flights and is a veteran of two NASA astrobiology missions chasing meteor storms around the Earth.

Joy S. Gaylinn Reidenberg (p. 165) is a professor of anatomy at the Icahn School of Medicine at Mount Sinai in New York City. She studies the bodies of humans and animals, and is the comparative anatomist for the TV show *Inside Nature's Giants* where she looks inside really big animals to see how their bodies work.

Mary Roach (p. 58) writes for *National Geographic*, *New Scientist*, *Wired* and the *New York Times*. Her books include *Gulp*, which takes a trip down your alimentary canal. She enjoys backpacking, Scrabble, mangoes and that Animal Planet show about horrific animals such as the parasitic worm that attaches itself to fishes' eyeballs.

Alice Roberts (p. 139) has always been fascinated by human anatomy and evolution. She currently teaches this subject at the University of Birmingham but also enjoys taking science to a wider audience: giving talks, writing books and presenting television programmes. Recent series on TV include *The Incredible Human Journey* and *Origins of Us*.

Tony Robinson (p. 9) is a presenter, actor and writer – a funny man who knows his history. He's well known for *Time Team* and as Baldrick in *Blackadder*, and his *Weird World of Wonders* history books for children have brought him yet another generation of fans.

Hans Rosling (p. 145) travels all over the place, asking questions about the state of health in the developing world. He's co-founder of the site Gapminder and likes to make things that seem boring, like statistics, interesting.

Tali Sharot (p. 208) is a neuroscientist (brain scientist) who examines how our emotions affect our behaviour and actions. She teaches at University College London, is often seen on TV and contributes to lots of magazines. She has recently written a book called *The Optimism Bias*.

Simon Singh (p. 39) wanted to be a nuclear physicist when he was nine. He studied particle physics and worked at Cambridge University and CERN, but realised he was better at writing about science than doing science. His books include *Big Bang*, *The Code Book*, *Fermat's Last Theorem* and *The Simpsons and Their Mathematical Secrets*.

Tom Smulders (p. 26) has been fascinated by animals since he was a child in Belgium, and knew he wanted to be a biologist from the age of ten. He now teaches biology and psychology to students at Newcastle University and investigates how titmice and magpies remember where they hid their food.

Paul Snelgrove (pp. 153, 189) explores the creatures living in the ocean. He's compiled a book chronicling a whopping 540 sea adventures, called *Discoveries of the Census of Marine Life*. If you look hard, you might find Nemo in there.

Dan Snow (p. 47) makes programmes about history for the BBC. He also writes books and iPad apps. He lives with his family and a giant Great Dane called Otto in the New Forest. Dan loves history because it includes the most exciting things that have ever happened to anyone ever.

Marcel Theroux (p. 184) is a broadcaster and award-winning novelist. His most recent novel is called *Strange Bodies*. His body's not strange at all though.

Jonathan R. Trappe (p. 99) holds the world record for longest flight by helium balloons: thirteen hours, thirty-six minutes and fifty-seven seconds over 109 miles, carried by fifty-seven balloons. He's also flown a house, just like Carl and Russell in the film *Up*, and hopes to cross the Atlantic by air in a lifeboat strung with hundreds of balloons.

Gabrielle Walker (pp. 193, 218) writes books and makes TV and radio programmes about the way the world works. She has swum with piranhas in the Amazon and used a hammer to pull lava out of a live volcano in Hawaii. Her latest book, *Antarctica*, is about her favourite place in the world, and she hopes it stays cold and icy for a long time to come.

Paul Watson (p. 206) and his friend Matthew had a mission: find the world's worst national football team and coach them to victory. Journalist Paul's book *Up Pohnpei* tells their amazing story.

Mike Webster (p. 94) spent many hours watching and playing around with animals as a child. He became a biologist so that he could carry on doing the same thing as a grown up. Being a biologist also means that he travels a lot and doesn't have to start work too early in the morning.

John Wells (p. 66) likes to study speech and sounds (he was Professor of Phonetics at University College London). John has written a dictionary about how to pronounce things, and enjoys singing and playing the melodeon, a type of accordion, in his spare time.

Ann Widdecombe (p. 57) used to be a Conservative politician. She's currently writing her fifth novel, *An Act of Brotherhood,* and enjoys spending time with her adopted goat Megan. Ann loves music but admits she's tone deaf.

Yan Wong (p. 129) is an evolutionary biologist and presenter on BBC1's *Bang Goes the Theory*, where he explains complicated stuff in a way that's easy to understand. His passion is biology and he helped write *The Ancestor's Tale* by Richard Dawkins.

Andrea Wulf (p. 49) wrote about the mad astronomers who criss-crossed the globe to observe the planets in her book *Chasing Venus*. Like them, she likes to travel the world but she's not quite made it to space.

Ilker Yilmaz (p. 122) holds one of the most bonkers world records ever. The Turkish construction worker can claim to have snorted milk up his nose then squirted it more than two metres out of his left eye. Please don't try this at home – or at school!

INDEX

universe: edge of, 2; number of galaxies, 2, 177–8; number of suns, 2

urine: drinking, 18; invisible ink, 39

vegetables: crying onions, 53; spicy chillies, 217; sweetcorn poo, 58–9

velociraptors, 32

Vikings, 134, 250

Vinci, Leonardo da: aeroplanes, 240; Mona Lisa, 62

voice, singing, 114

vulture, wing bones and musical instruments, 10

water, as fuel for cars, 51–2

weather: on Moon, 242; rainbows, 204–5

Wenlock, Olympic mascot, 284

whales: communication, 67; farting, 165; shark, 247–8; size, 129–30

world: largest country of, 241; population of, 145–6; smallest island nation of, 255; *see also* Earth

worms, 259

Wright brothers, the, 239–40

yawning, 42–3

zebras, 54–5

Out Now in Paperback

WHY CAN'T I TICKLE MYSELF?

Big Questions from Little People
Answered by Some Very Big People

'An invaluable spur to asking questions and thinking
about answers.' *Guardian*

'The whole family will be hooked.'
Sunday Times Style magazine